MILLION DOLLAR SECRETS FOR REAL ESTATE MARKETING & SALES

THE KEY TO HOW BROKERS, REALTORS AND AGENTS CAN GAIN 10X INCOME

Published in the United States by The Million Dollar Book Club.

ISBN: 978-1-945196-05-8

jebdurgin.com

themilliondollarbookclub.com

Dedication

My friend once told me the definition of Kung-Fu is any
discipline or skill achieved through hard work and practice.
Heck, if that were true, most entrepreneurs we would be
considered deadly weapons. But are we? I feel like many
of us are black belts in rehearsal, but amateurs on fight
night. This book is dedicated to those entrepreneurs taking
action, those that show up when it really counts. They are
not sitting on the sidelines where it is safe, but instead are
right in the thick of it: they are the ones taking roundhouses
to the head but keep on fighting. Never get comfortable and
be in the thick of it, no matter how hard you get hit.
Remember: COMFORT IS THE SILENT THIEF.

I want to give a very special thank you to my good friend
and mentor Chief Denney. He's a genuine guy that will do
almost anything for anyone looking to better themselves. I
also want to say thanks to Jorge Olson & MDBC, Dave
Stech & MGM, the 10x group, all those who have pushed
me along the way and my parents for dealing with me
always going against the grain. Thank you all for pulling
me up to a higher level.

TABLE OF CONTENTS

Introduction

The real estate marketing business is a vibrant and competitive one. There are real estate agents who survive the tides, while others will exit even before they see their second or third anniversary. To keep your head above water as an agent in the real estate business, you may need to change your tactics and employ different strategies. A question I hear often is "what is the secret for success in selling real estate?" It's no surprise to me people are asking this kind of question over and over again.

What I would like to emphasize is real estate marketing many times is mistaken to be about the "property"— selling a home, condo, or apartment, or whatever asset type it may be. While the ultimate goal may be to sell the property, they agent needs to realize to be able to identify the traps, inconsistencies and mistakes that could easily derail their efforts and ambitions, thereby ultimately plunging them into a dark pit in their business endeavors.

If you plan to join the real estate selling business or you already are doing it, there are certain things that are the non-negotiables, the things you have to do right. No doubt about it— it's either you get it right, or you're swept away by the raging tide. That's why you see majority of agents either closing their doors or others clinging onto the plank waiting for their last dive. Nonetheless, there are a tiny number of agents who continue to keep afloat and have managed to stay in the business.

In this book, I will identify and examine some of these tactics in the real estate business and will identify if agents are doing them right or wrong. This is ultimately where you see the rubber meets the road, either you do it right, or you don't do it at all.

As an investor, I often put myself in the shoes of a client: a home buyer or a home seller.

During my time in real estate marketing, I have identified new trends and activities, which I may openly say are the most devastating to new agents, and which often are the root cause of failure in this business. If real estate agents are able to reposition themselves and do just a few things different, they would probably be reaping huge returns and would be enjoying the fruits of their labor.

Why I Have Written This Book

I have written this book because there is a huge void needing to be filled in real estate marketing and sales. After working closely with agents for some time now, I am consistently seeing ordinary things—ordinary marketing and ordinary sales strategies. Real estate professionals are using the same marketing, strategies and tactics that were introduced years ago. So, they are getting the same results. Think of it this way, if you were to start a business, you will also come up with strategies to run it. But, you will find that a couple of years later, the market dimensions will change including customer buying behavior. You either adapt or your business will die.

If you continue to cling on to the same outdated strategies, you may find you aren't getting results, and if you are, they are just similar results year in and year out. I'm assuming the main reason you are in the real estate market is to grow big; not just about making ordinary money but earning big money. That means you will constantly need to employ different tactics in real estate marketing or selling. This is, however, not happening with the majority of Realtors I have seen or engaged with. That's why these Realtors are getting similar results year in and year out.

Realtors need a game-changer this time around so they tap into the huge potential that's in the market. Unless there is a shift in the way agents conduct their marketing, they aren't going to see any increase in earnings they make.

What Realtors are getting is ordinary results from ordinary selling tactics. Everything is just ordinary and that's why they are getting results that are outdated. These are results that were expected ten-years ago. These tactics are not what is needed in today's age to get ahead of the curve.

My aim of creating this book is actually to enable you (the Brokers, Realtors and Agents) to create your own curve. I will give you the tools to stop being a forager of what is already created by real estate professionals in the past and start doing things differently. This book will allow you to break free of the old marketing cliché you're entangled in, and will get you thinking and acting different.

You may find that a Realtor who does things different easily makes Money. But there is another agent in the same market who is finding it very difficult to make money.

If you are making sixty to eighty thousand-dollars a year, you could probably double, triple, or grow that tenfold. I will show you how you can turn around your earnings, salary, commission, or profit into ten times more. That's what I am trying to accomplish with writing this book.

I want the people using this book to be nowhere near the competition. After reading this book, I want others in your industry to look at you and say: *"That guy is doing ten times what I'm doing; I want to know what the secret is!."* Everything is going to be different (as you shall discover when you read the book), *especially* your real estate marketing and sales.

Who Should Read This Book

Anyone who wants to get to the next level in real estate marketing is a perfect fit to read this book. You may ask: what do you mean *"Next level"*? By this I mean any person who aspires to venture into real estate selling or anyone who is already in the business, but has not made significant strides in growing. They wouldn't want to miss reading or listening to this book— it's a complete game changer.

If you feel like you are stuck or just making circles in your current business without seeing any significant growth in your customer base, profits, and returns on investment, you MUST read this book. Even if you consider yourself to be one of the smartest in the industry, this book will give you extreme value!

You will be surprised how you will be able to turn things around just by following the steps, ideas, suggestions, strategies, and selling methods that are discussed herein.

The book is created for Agents, Realtors and Brokers; but the methods can really be applied to anyone in the real estate industry that wants to create real success rather than relying on others to give it to them.

Often times, we think that someone else's tactics are the best— simply because they are spending huge amounts on marketing or putting their big images on benches. The notion is that, "If that guy can afford to put their ads on every other bench in the city, they must be doing it right." It's hard for us to break out of the norm because we are scared, and don't want to try something else, or something new. We don't know whether it is proven or not. It is this fear that makes us operate in the ordinary sphere. As they always say: what's the difference between ordinary and extra-ordinary? That little bit extra. This book will give you that little bit extra.

People who are the best in almost any industry are at the forefront of trying something new. So, what has been working in this industry may be what worked in the past but it's not geared towards getting to the next level. The real estate industry is a very unique business, which needs unique selling strategies. That's what is lacking and needs to be introduced.

Someone who reads, comprehends, understands, and applies the knowledge and strategies in this book will be able to build and grow their earnings tenfold. All the suggestions are most applicable for the real estate market, but I believe can be applied to many industries.

BEFORE YOU GET STARTED READING:

My suggestion is to write down your annual income today and put it on the front page of this book. One year from now, when you look to see what you have earned, my goal for you is to be writing down an income that is at *least* double (or even more) than what you originally wrote down. So, the new "normal" is going to be double your income.

I have talked a lot on "normal", "ordinary", or "same." And I have said that Realtors are doing and following normal behaviors. They want to follow the path of normal. They don't want to change, that's why they are getting normal results. But that's not what I want Realtors to attain by reading this book. So, I think it is first important to identify what is "normal" so you will know if you're stuck in the thick of it!

Typical Results

What's Normal Earnings for A Real Estate Agent

What does a real estate agent or Realtor make in a year? According to NAR it's something around seventy-five thousand-dollars nationally and locally (referring to San Diego) it is about sixty-eight thousand-dollars. Couple this number with the research I conducted identifying agents are only going to spend about two hours at most a week on education, reading, and learning and you should realize this is the same as dying slowly. It's just enough for you to say: But it's enough to keep a roof over my family and enough to keep us content. Horse crap. I want you to be able to provide a roof for every family member. I don't want content; I want you to have a life you would have only dreamed of in the past!

The first thing is to identify why this trend in education should not be acceptable to you. When you look at what research reveals about reading and studying, you find that the performing CEO's in most any industry read up to sixty books in a year. These are business books, which of course, are quite shorter than a novel— probably about half the content in a novel. But still sixty books aren't something little— it's a TON of material to study. Keep in mind, these guys are very busy, way busier then you or I. They are heads of fortune companies.

So, when a broker tries to use the excuse: I don't have time to read. Then they must be making ten million, twenty million, or a hundred million dollars a year! Why? Because that's the only way they could be that busy. But the reality is that the people who make this kind of money read and study around the clock. So, one may ask, "When do these big earners have time to work, if they only read and study most of the time?"

According to research, the best paid agents in 2013 were paid ninety-eight thousand-dollars, the average real estate broker or agent made about thirty-nine thousand and the lowest paid group made twenty-one thousand-dollars in that year. If you're working the whole day and have no time to read because you are so busy, and you are the one only making twenty-one thousand-dollars a year, it means something is definitely wrong. This means if you were to double your earnings you still would not even get close to the top of the earning group. You probably need to do plus five or ten times more in order to get somewhere closer to the top. I would say if you're making twenty-one thousand-dollars and claim to be busy, you're only going around in circles. That's what they call "busy work" rather than productive work. It's time to change it up!

What Is the Average Number of Transactions?

A real estate agent does about four to six transactions in a year. On a quota basis, someone who is only doing four to six transactions a year while working for a boss would likely be fired. How do you do one transaction in a span of three months? It means there must be something you aren't doing correct. And yes, this includes agents who only work part-time on nights and weekends. It is still unacceptable.

I feel like part of the problem may be they don't have a direct boss leaning over their shoulder, they have no one to be pushing them to meet targets. While this may be a problem, I still believe there is more to it than that, which is resulting to only six transactions a year, at most.

In every business, there are systems and virtues put in place to make a difference. Top performing professionals in any industry have rituals, virtues, and schedules, which they stick to. They do this so they don't have to rely on someone else to tell them what to do. This allows them make it to the next level. It is something that pushes them to meet a goal or a target. This set of systems or rituals can be called a business practice or a marketing plan.

Business practices or a marketing plan tells you what you need to do when you wake up in the morning instead of wondering, "What am I doing to do now?", "Am I going

17

knocking on doors?", "Am I going to make calls?", This should not be how your day starts. You may be thinking: yea right, my day is more like what fires do I have to put out today, or I don't have time to think, I only have time to react. WRONG AGAIN.

You want to be in a situation where when you wake up in the morning, you know that "I have to make fifty-three calls today, or I'm knocking on seventeen doors today." A very strategic plan that you stick to, one that generates results!

The system or plan will tell you what you should be doing on a daily basis. Yes, fires will need to be put out, but you can't be running a business shooting from the hip. Your shots need to be calculated and well thought out. Make every one of them count. It's much more effective and delivers a heavier punch using this strategy. Don't worry, we will help you create this plan later in the book.

What are the Average Earning and Transactions in a specific market: San Diego, CA

San Diego is one of the largest cities in the country with a vibrant real estate market. Yes, its neighbor Los Angeles gets far more attention, but San Diego still holds its own in many aspects.

In the real estate market, you will see it is very volatile and has a hyper competitive market. The average transactions are only about four to six transactions in a year. The average earnings, commission, or salary for a Realtor is about sixty-eight thousand-dollars annually. For a state that charges a tax for almost everything, including the local San Diego running joke of also paying a "sunshine tax", this simply will not do. It's just not enough to extraordinary life where you can provide for all the people you love and care about.

The average amount of education spent on education on a weekly basis by real estate agents is sad: about an hour and usually it's only because it is required of them. It's typically work related around some sort of meeting or discussions regarding the state of the real estate market.

This is the amount of education a typical real estate agent probably gets. Basically, there is no education for real estate agents when it comes to self-development. These are the same professionals who are closing one house per quarter.

When an agent takes the strategies provided in this book and applies them correctly, they could probably make what they are making in an entire year in just one month. This turns around everything in the real estate selling business—were talking about making real progress on your financial future.

Imagine you earn an annual commission of forty thousand-dollars and after months of practicing better and effective client-oriented real estate selling, you are able to earn a commission of forty thousand-dollars a month (not a year). And this is on the low end— doing only six transactions in a year. That's unbelievable!

And yes, I know what you're saying: but I don't need that much money, I just need enough many so I can spend time with my family and do the occasional vacation to Disneyland. Listen up: making these changes will allow you to spend all the time you want with your family. Forget just looking forward to the weekends. Rather than just taking the kids, you're now flipping the bill so the entire family reunion is hosted at Disneyland.

An example of a top performing agent in San Diego:

Let's put a yardstick on real estate selling in San Diego. When I look at the real estate market, I can say that I personally know a top performing agent that put down one thousand, nine hundred and twenty-eight transactions in one year!! This is an agent with an accolade that allows her to be featured in the *Wall Street Journal* as among the leading real estate agents nationwide and not just in San Diego.

But what makes her shine in an otherwise six-transaction-a-year market? Being in the real estate selling industry, as large as it is, is pretty a small one. When you get to know people in the industry, word spreads fast.

I have a close friend and mentor who put me in touch with this top performing agent. I wanted to talk to a professional who has been in the industry, and knew the market where I was selling a house. Now keep in mind, I'm not a large investor by any means, and do not deserve any special treatment. But I want you to pay attention to how she handled our interaction. Also, keep in mind she is a very busy woman, I mean common-she did *thousands* of transactions in one year!

Now keep in mind, she is used to taking care of people who come to her with multiple houses they want to sell, I wanted to sell ONE. When I contacted her, obviously I knew who I was speaking to, but most impressively: she knew who I was. I didn't even have time to introduce myself— she answered the phone by saying: .

"Jeb, is that you? And caught off guard, I asked her: "How did you know my name?", she said," I been expecting your call. I'm in the middle of a meeting right now, but if this important, I can step out, otherwise may I call you back in just a few moments?"

At that very moment in time, I knew why she is the best in the industry. Imagine this, I am calling someone I haven't talked to before in my life, using out of state unidentified phone number and she already knows my name—not only that she takes the time to answer the phone in the middle of a meeting! I think this is something very few agents are doing in this industry.

The Realtor took the time to find out who I was and better yet; I don't know what kind of a meeting she was in, but she paused everything and everyone around her to let me know I was the most important thing going on in her life at that moment.

Now I realize you may not have seen into it as deeply as I did, but keep in mind, this was no coincidence. She takes the time to answer the call no matter how little a client is. From the moment she picked up the phone, calling me by my name and even the hushed I'm-not-supposed-to-be-talking-to-you tone of her voice during the conversation, it made a great impact on the client. This shows me she is a well-educated real estate professional who has probably read many many books on customer relationship management and knows how to make clients feel important— because this is exactly how I felt from that first encounter on the phone. This is a person who practices, learns, and studies that kind of relationship building, because it doesn't just happen automatically and that was not fluke.

Unless you have read widely and understand what it takes to relate with your clients, you probably cannot do what she did in her first encounter on phone with me in just a few moments. You may be thinking: yea I can! Oh really? You would have taken an out of state phone call during the middle of one of your meetings when you're sitting with someone right in front of you? While the common thought is: well that's just rude understand this: it was not rude because she likely told others before the meeting: "I want to apologize in advance, I may have to take a call during this meeting". Planned, precise and calculated to sound like a random act but really was exactly the first impression she wanted to make.

That in itself shows she knows what she is doing in real estate selling. This is what it takes to be a top performing agent.

Now you have begun to see how the ones moving the needle in this industry do things a bit differently. It's very important to begin by at least identifying if you are in fact the average agent yielding typical results. If you don't know you're the average, how do you suppose you are to improve? Let's look just a little closer at ordinary before we make the changes to become extraordinary.

What Are the Typical Marketing Campaigns Real Estate Agents Use?

Some of the common marketing campaigns real estate agents use (and they think they are smart) are things like business cards, flyers, billboards, bench ads, postcards, radio ads, websites, YouTube videos, and photographs. In fact, much of the photography they utilize is simply a picture of them. The whole branding idea of real estate agents is, just talking about them. That's the message they are sending across: "it's all about me", "I am an agent", "Hey, it's me the agent".

What realtors may not be aware of is real estate selling is not about "me", but about "you" the client or the buyer. It's neither about "me" meaning the agent nor about "the house" meaning the product. It's much more to do with the clients and how you, as an agent relate with them. Agents that think of themselves as "the smart ones" market on benches, get on radio, use billboards and send out videos and photographs, but is that all? Those very same agents tell the client, "Choose me because I'm on radio", or "Who does Real Estate better than me, I'm featured on TV, I am the guy!"

What I presume is even those pushing the ads are typical, they aren't doing anything atypical. And the key takeaway you must understand is the typical mindset earns your typical earnings. The idea is, if you do what everyone is doing, you get exactly what should be expected. You will make the seventy thousand-dollars a year every other "smart" real estate agent would make. But should things be done that way in the real estate business? They may be the leaders by virtue of the money they spend on things like radio ads, but soon enough the market may show them the door.

Let's look at the ways we can stay in the market for a very long period of time. How we can change the ordinary selling strategies into something much less ordinary. As an agent, you should really be asking yourself one key question: how can I turn one customer into one hundred customers? The answer is much simpler then you may think: treat this business like what it is; a marketing business rather than the real estate business.

A New Way of Thinking

Do the numbers and think like a marketer

When you are in the business of real estate selling, you want to, *"do the numbers and think like a marketer."* By this, I don't mean reaching your goal numbers; I mean do the numbers like a marketer. Contrary to popular belief, this is not real estate business but a marketing business! True success in real estate selling comes from success in real estate marketing. If we want to think like a marketer, we will be marketing homes, people, agents, and all other real estate discourse, so it's one hundred percent marketing.

The first big take-away I would like to share with you is this: if you can't measure it, it's not marketing. That is exactly what I mean when I say *"do the numbers and think like a marketer,"* You should understand how direct response works. For instance, I need to know if I spend one dollar will I make one dollar twenty-five cents in return. If I spend two dollars' will I make three dollars back? With this in mind, you can increase or reduce your budget. This way, you can measure it. The underlying idea here is: can you measure the results?

If you put an ad on paper and give your direct cell phone number, you won't be able to measure that. Why? That's your personal number and everyone calls you through that number. You won't be able to know how many people called to inquire more about that specific house or from a specific ad. There are friends who call you, family members will call, and perhaps a few clients may call. Simply put, if everyone is calling you on that same phone number, it is nearly impossible for you to measure the marketing results. But if you put an advertisement for a house on paper and give a specific phone number dedicated for that ad only, you will then be able to know how many people called as a result of that very specific ad for that very specific property... You can say, "Three people called", "ten people called", or "no one called." All those calling the dedicated number for that specific marketing channel have an interest in a specific property.

In real estate selling, measuring is everything. A lot of people tend to think marketing is hard work. That's the perception. But truth be told; marketing is statistics, it's math, it's boring math, unless you put the symbol "$" On it, then it's sexy. Otherwise, real estate selling is just about numbers. Hence, in this lesson, we learn that in real estate marketing, you have to measure everything. You have to quantify everything you do. If you advertise on radio or any type of advertising channel like TV, you have to measure it. You are not Coca-Cola; you are not in the branding business but selling industry, meaning you have to measure the results of every single dollar.

At this stage, in order to understand how much, we should be spending on marketing and in what specific marketing avenues, it's important to identify what a customer is worth.

Average value of a customer

An important thing every person in real estate selling should know is the average value of a customer. How much money will be made from a customer in one sale and then again in a life time? Think of a typical home price— it costs on average four hundred-thousand-dollars. If you are an agent, and you sell one house, you will likely get a typical commission of two point five percent, that's roughly about, if not precise, ten-thousand-dollars. Ten thousand dollars is the average value of one customer. Now, as a real estate agent, that's the number you associate with the client: This client is worth ten-thousand dollars to me.

But, there is also something else very interesting here, and it is very important for you to grasp, so pay attention. To you, that client is worth a ten-thousand-dollar commission, but the question is: what does the home seller think you are worth? Four hundred-thousand-dollars. Now, you see, there is a very different view of the same transaction among both you. The customer (or home seller) sees you as a four hundred-thousand-dollars person, and you see the client as a ten-thousand-dollars person. This is very important you realize this when you are speaking with the clients.

Life time value of a customer

In a lifetime, let's say that same homeowner sends you two referrals. That means you will get another twenty-thousand-dollars from the two referrals they sent with a transactional value of eight hundred-thousand-dollars (based on the average home sale of four-hundred thousand dollars). In a lifetime, that one customer is now worth a thirty-thousand-dollar commission to you with a total transactional value of one point two-million-dollars. Do you see how we arrived at those figures?

The thirty-thousand-dollar commission is arrived by adding the commission earned by the customer of ten-thousand-dollars plus the twenty-thousand-dollars commission earned from the two referrals he sent to you since the original transaction. Since each transactional value (average home sales price) is worth four hundred-thousand-dollars, it means that the lifetime transaction value of that one customer is one point two-million dollars. (meaning four hundred-thousand-dollars multiplied by three: the customers plus the two referrals). This is what that customer is worth to your real estate selling business in a lifetime, and this changes the game completely.

Let's use a goal of five transactions in one year, all coming from one client. While this assumption is an atypical one, it's what we would like clients to do. Let's say the client brings us one referral per year for the next five years. In this case, one customer bringing one transaction every year for five years equals fifty-thousand dollars. We are also looking at one customer who is bringing two million dollars in sales.

What do you do for a customer who brings in five referrals over five years adding up to a commission of fifty-thousand-dollars and a transaction value of two million dollars? Before you answer that, let's begin with a typical response. Let me put myself in the shoes of a customer: I send you two million dollars' worth of business and you send me a thank you card with a plastic gift card in it? It's a slap on the face!

Investing in our customers

Things need to change; we need to invest something more than an occasional gift card in our customers. Here, we are going to do the marketing numbers. Or in other words, what dollar amount we should invest in these customers. Remember that a home buyer can potentially buy several houses and the probability is they will use the same Realtor (as long as you did a half-decent job) in their future purchases. But do Realtors see this potential and how to connect with the home buyers to ensure they are retained, and feel appreciated for seeking services from same Realtor again and again? From my experience, it doesn't look like the case.

How much are realtors investing in selling a house?

Let's begin by looking at the typical investment by a Realtor when marketing a home to sell. What's the percentage agents should invest when marketing a home or property? I will tell you, if you ask an agent this question, you will be shocked. They don't have a percentage. Most Realtors won't give you a direct answer. It's usually a "more then I should have" type of answer. In short, they do not measure, so they do not have the figures. That's because they don't know up front what they are committed to spending on marketing a house.

I had to do some digging myself to find out what agents actually spend on marketing a home for their customers. Typically, I found they spend less than half a percent! Hell, they didn't even know what figures to quote when I asked them this exact question: "Exactly how much money or what percentage do you spend in marketing a home for sale?" I had to measure for them based on the numbers I got from a few examples of past sales.

Here is one of those examples: I sold a home for three hundred and eighty-thousand-dollars through an agent and when I asked the agent how much he had spent on marketing, he told me about one thousand, eight hundred-dollars. (Which I was actually surprised he knew that number…That's not usually the case) He was spending money on fliers, pictures, websites, and YouTube videos. The agent was doing whatever everyone else is doing. Now keep in mind, half of that amount goes to paying for a professional photographer! (As it should, because this is one area you CANNOT cut corners on).

The thing is, most agents don't even consider documenting they are driving to the house using gas. They don't measure the amount of time it took the assistant to help with the copied papers, the cost of balloons for the open house, etc. All of that doesn't count to them, but they need those figures to know how much they spend on marketing a home for sale. And while you may think: well yea, but I can't tell me client I'm using gas money as part of the money used to market their home, the answer is this: you better! If my realtor not only told me exactly what he spent down to the dollar, but also included the gas money and other items, he could likely prove to me he spent nearly his whole commission! Now keep in mind, the investment the agents are making should be directly impacting the leads of the house so know what you can feasibly push as an expense here, no need to start pushing it. Remember, identifying this information actually benefits your knowledge of your own business much more than the client.

The whole business of agents selling homes boils down to one thing— measuring results. A Realtor must commit a percentage of their commission- Let's say one percent, five percent, hell 50%...Whatever it is, it needs to be measured in detail.

Now, let's measure another aspect of this business, the business of customer relationship management. This would include looking at the kind of gifts or incentives agents give to invest into their customers, especially the ones that bring us multiple deals! In the first ten houses I sold, what was the typical gift from an agent? You guessed it--- I received a thank you card. (Sometimes I would score big with a $10 or $20 Starbucks card..yay)

What are some of the gifts typical agents give to their customer?

You may tend to think a customer who gets you more business should also be appreciated and recognized for that work. That customer should get more incentives or rewards as a way of saying thank you because he or she has given you additional opportunities. But from my own observation, it's actually the opposite. They give me less attention even after selling ten homes, because they know I will be bringing more opportunities. They actually tend to pay more attention to the first-time client.

Outside of a Thank you card and occasional gift card, I have only received one other present— a bottle of wine, and it wasn't even a nice one for that matter. (About a $30 bottle)

After bringing tons of business to you, I only get a bottle of wine? (Which If he would have asked he would have found out I don't like wine) He couldn't even bring a bottle of Champagne? That's what the typical present will be, and you bet your ass it's not enough. If I had something like a one-hundred-dollar bill folded in a thank you card, I could probably buy a decent bottle of champagne if that is the best they can give me. But this is like zero.

The agent was kind enough to hand deliver the bottle of wine at one of my houses and I remember him standing there and he was like "You can open it!" I thought what am I going to open this bottle of wine with? Surely, he could have given me a bottle opener…but no, he didn't. So now I need to go buy a bottle opener so I can share it with you? By the way, it was a $32 bottle of warm white wine (he was classy enough to leave the price tag on the bottle). You know the worst thing about this? This was actually a bit out of the ordinary; this was like over-the-top for realtor customer satisfaction standards. This was the best gift I had ever received from ANY of my realtors.

What I'm trying to get at is agents need to discover better ways of saying "Thank you" to their customers. They need to think of things out of the ordinary. For example, they can consider creative ideas like buying a customer something for their new house (either the one they are buying, or the new one they are moving into after selling their old one). It may be a coffee table, an appliance like a microwave, or even a stainless steel bar-b-q. To put it simple, home buyers need more than a "cheap bottle of wine" to say: *Thank You*! It's got to be more than a Thank you card that always ends with asking for another referral. It has to be done a different way.

How much money to spend on a client

Agents need to assign a budget. For example, they can say "I'm going to spend ten percent of my commission on this client" because that will turn my one commission into five.

Think like this: If I earn ten-thousand-dollars from this client in a year and allocate two thousand-dollars to that client in thoughtful gifts, he is going to want to give me more business! If an agent invests two thousand-dollars for a year or two on the client, he is bound to earn fifty-thousand-dollars. That's a good investment; I guarantee it's a better investment than door hangers. This is a goal you are setting. You will not do it bare handed— not with a bottle of wine, and certainly not with just a thank you card, but going an extra mile to offer something appreciable and memorable. This time around you will show the agent really cares for that two million dollars' worth of transactional value the client brings.

Other places Agents are falling short:

The follow up

The follow up is the most sensitive thing for a real estate agent. Consider this for example; after somebody sells a house, do you stay in touch with them? Do you call them every week, month, or year? What do you do with that customer? Is there any follow up with this important client making you fifty-thousand-dollars in five years? (Remember our example of one transaction per year for five years) These are the questions you should be asking yourself as an agent.

In my view, follow up in the real estate selling business is dead— it's not in existence. This is where there is a huge gap that needs to be filled. There is a void in follow up, simply put. And, if there is anything we can call "follow up" that agents do (and for that matter the ones we are calling "smart" agents), it is just what we already talked about— the Thank you card.

This is what they get after putting our trust in someone that guides us though one of the biggest financial decisions we have made in our lifetime? Pretty much nothing at all. Perhaps if a customer is lucky, may be on Christmas, an anniversary, or on a birthday they may get something else. But it's still going to be a card, and you bet your ass it's always going to end with asking for more business: "your greatest compliment is a referral" I'm so sick of seeing that.

To put it blatantly, the agent is saying, "Happy Birthday! By the way, I could always use more money from you"

There are actually a few Realtors who have performed the follow up over a phone call as opposed to a card. the disappointing thing is that it was not that they were checking with me to see if I am happy with the home or with life in general. They simply said: Hi Jeb! Do you have intentions of buying more houses have anyone you can refer to me that does want to sell or buy a home? Yea, sure let me send you more money so I can get the crappy card! Now I'm not new to this, I realize this is business and this is how's it's always been done, so sack up and quite wining. Right?

Well, I'm telling you now, if you were to call and invite me over for a couple beers and to watch the fight on HBO I would have a much different feeling. Even if I denied the option of going for whatever reason (which by the way, don't you think if you were to ask me those same exact questions about more business while I'm sipping a cold

beer with your id be much more apt to doing business)
What If you were to invite me to go to the Chargers
football game in town? (Which I've always secretly wanted
to do) in the real estate business this does not happen. It's
obvious they don't want to hang out, what they are
concerned about is getting more of my money, or sending
them someone else they can get money from. It's all about
them not about me, the client.

You might be thinking: well Jeb, you're an investor. What
about the number of calls you get from agents all saying
they have a house that's going to make *you* money if you
buy it through them? The answer is simple: it hardly
happens. Like almost never. Many of the agents are more
interested in selling the house I have already renovated. I
get it, you want the silver platter with the steak already
cooked, but you don't want anything to do with hunting
this beast down. What I really want to point out is that of
the very few agents that call me with a "deal", many of
them are not educated enough to know what a good deal is.
Many times whatever they are thinking is going to make
me money, isn't actually going to make me money at all.
The agents think that it will; they call me excited, but what
I have come to find out is that, they don't understand the
mechanism of it. They haven't done enough education on
their side to know what constitutes an actual deal.

Yes, yes. You call me because I'm the investor, you're the
realtor. You bring me the lead and I determine if it's a deal
that will work for me or not. But think of it like this: If an

agent called me and rather then ask me how they can get my listings, or what I thought of any of the hundreds of auto-forward properties the criteria that took them all of 5 minutes to set up on MLS, they asked me how they can be educated enough to know a good deal when they see one. Honestly, if they called and said those simple words, they would probably get all my listings.

Why? Because I can tell they are interested in the longevity of building our business together! They want to know how my business works, so they can grow it as well. Plus, if the property doesn't work for me, they will know exactly what information another investor will be looking for when they send them the deal! Currently, agents just call me to see if they can make more money by listing my properties. Typical nonsense. And my typical answer for them: stand in line.

What about the referrals…are there any follow ups?

What is the amount of money agents give to their customers for referrals? This is a difficult issue because of the legality aspect of it. I partially don't want to talk about it because of the nature of the topic. However, we all know there are ways to work with great clients and as long as you have a little bit of creativity, everyone will walk away happy.

Imagine if a Realtor had called a past client and offered to send the person to a place like Hawaii, or, give a bathroom remodel as a gift in exchange for referrals? That doesn't happen. It's the typical thing… a Thank you card and likely the comment about asking for more referrals. What this tells me is that the industry is open to make a lot of money if agents do things right. Meaning if they do things different from the typical agent, they can crush it!

Developing a Marketing Plan

The customer is the most important person in a real estate, treat them that way. A real estate agent should always be staying in touch with their customers and the people those clients refer. Keeping in contact with the clients will create a lasting bond that is bound to yield results. The "Follow up" is something every Realtor should consider serious. This follow-up should have a budget. The budget is for their marketing activity that includes the development around nurturing customers. A Realtor needs to know exactly how much they are going to spend on each customer or with other business professionals they may deal with.

It is said a typical home buyer will purchase a new home every 5 to 7 years and if you use your marketing correctly, that same customer will refer you other customers. Then, there are also everyday people we will run into in this business like electricians, plumbers, carpenters, cleaners, home designers, builders, home appraisers, and other people who provide services to homeowners. All of these people and services form a key element in the real estate selling business.

Therefore, a Realtor needs to budget for these people so that he or she knows how much to gift them when they refer a customer to buy a house. Think of it like this: you can either spend money on typical marketing, or you can spend money on alternative marketing (hooking people up). Don't you think the unexpected gifts these people receive are better spent then throwing the same amount of money towards traditional marketing? I can tell you one thing, it feels waayyy better making someone smile with delight and seeing the reaction on their face in person rather than writing out and then mailing a check to someone I've never even met for marketing.

Allocating a certain percentage of the commission to use on these people will ensure these people will be pumped to see you! Heck, the only other person sending people gifts like this is Either Santa Claus or Oprah. (And look how successful they are!) This allocated fund will foster success in the real estate selling business.

The "marketing" fund is spent on things like newsletters, taking customers on vacations, involving them in sports events, live concerts, or even hosting barbecues. The thing is; realtors avoid these avenues because it's not traditional marketing. Guess what: it's typical. For heaven's sake, please don't send a postcard saying "your biggest compliment to me is a referral." Hand deliver the Lakers tickets and say "your biggest compliment to me is to join my courtside!"

By this point in time, you may be thinking to yourself: "Okay, this all sounds great Jeb, but how do you achieve all this? How do you know how often and how much to allocate?"

Don't worry, I got you. You will need to come up with a system or a plan to help you figure this out. A marketing plan is the building block for your real estate selling business. Here is a step by step guideline on how to develop your marketing plan. Let's first start with your personal marketing before talking about your business marketing.

How to Start Creating Personal Marketing:

Step 1: Have A Luring Elevator Speech or Pitch

What I have realized is when most realtors meet customers, they want show they are real estate agents with a business card. However, everyone already knows a realtor; so what are you doing differently? This first impression is where your "elevator speech" can absolutely destroy your competition.

An elevator speech is a brief speech you use to spark or captivate interest of people on your brand, product, service, or you. It shouldn't take more than thirty-seconds (the time it takes for an elevator to take you from the top of a building to the bottom— hence its name.) Ill share with you a really efficient one-page PDF version I use to help craft this elevator pitch. This elevator pitch is key to marketing yourself as different from the pack.

In the elevator pitch, you want to deliver a brief description highlighting who you are and what you do. This needs to captivate interest with the customer or person you're talking to. In this brief introduction, you have to deliver a message that has an effect on them so much that they say, "Holy cow, we need to talk more; this is exactly what I've been looking for! Let me have your business card!" or "I have just the person you need to meet."

Now, look at the way they responded to what you said. All you have told them is that you are a realtor (one of many they likely already know) in that thirty-second elevator pitch, but because the way it was crafted you're the only one they are thinking of.

Step 2: Create A Short "About Me" Video

Heaven forbid you don't get a chance to deliver the power punch elevator pitch in person. What's a great way to still deliver a similar message? Create a short video! Not all times a Realtor will be meeting face-to-face with customers or people. A short video about you as a Realtor can make a huge difference. The benefit of this video can be even better than the real life version. Why? Lighting, make-up rehearsal, sprinkled with some of your own personal flare will allow this detailed and thought out personal version may actually be even more effective than the marketing mixer elevator pitch.

I would actually encourage you to do one more version of your elevator pitch: from your phone on the run. Why would you do one on the fly? Why have the dog, cat, distractions? Because it's real life. We get along with other people when we can relate to them. Things like having animals running around in the background, kids jumping in the swimming pool, and the neighbor mowing all at the same time si exactly what we can relate to. Use your real life as the perfect backdrop for your very "un-scripted" video (yet you and I know your elevator pitch has been memorized)….because that is who you are! You are parents, husbands, neighbors, etc. and we all like these people in our lives because we are also those people!

You email right? Send this video in your email signature! This is not going to be just the typical boring email signature: Jeb Durgin, Keller Williams licensed Realtor, blah blah. It has all that same information, but at the bottom it will say:

"Before you Google me or look at my LinkedIn or Facebook page, click here to find out more about me!" and that you hyperlink to your you tube page is your way to get them to watch not only your elevator pitch, but all your additional videos with you talking about the client and your business can help them solve problems.

In the video, you can say, "Hey, this is me (your name), your best resource for real estate solutions" and then talk about something with the business this time. Talk about what you do in this business and ensure that it is not something everyone else is doing. It is this difference or uniqueness you tell the people through the video that entices them to want to know more about you. Wrap it up with something personal, reason being, people want to know about you. People want to know who you are outside of business and how that connects with them on personal and business level.

You can even put that elevator speech on CDs and distribute to people. This can also be packaged in a referral program where in addition to giving handouts and newsletters, you also have the CDs containing the elevator pitch.

So, if it's not obvious so far, when you are creating your marketing plan, one of the most important things is to make sure you have ways to impress people, ways that are not normal. Now that we have talked very briefly about just a couple personal marketing strategies, let's talk about business marketing:

How to Start Creating a Business Marketing Plan

Let's break down our marketing plan so you know how to go about creating it. This is going to be a marketing plan template you can use to guide you in coming up with the steps to follow. Grab a piece of paper, a tablet, smartphone, or PC, and let's start writing your marketing plan.

Let's start with the content of the marketing plan with the most important priorities:

Content of a marketing plan

1. Personal Goals— what do you want to achieve? For example, "I want to make a million dollars' profit by August 21st, 2025." This would be a very specific personal goal you want to achieve. When you do your marketing plan, you will keep this financial goal in mind

2. Target Market—*Who* is your ideal client? In this section of the book, I will touch on the avatar questionnaire. An avatar is your ideal client. You will have an 'avatar questionnaire' that allows you to

identify who/what/why that client is and how we can learn to market very specifically to them.

3. How to attract new business- you want to know the strategies to use to get new business

4. The follow up strategy for new leads and existing customers

The budget— the percentage you are going to put back in the business for marketing such as for gifts, vacation, hosting barbecues, and such other activities or events.

Goal Setting

Setting Goals

An author once said *"A person without a goal is like a ship without a destination. You're simply at the mercy of the sea"* Without clearly set goals, you would have no idea if you're where you should be at any given time.

Before we go deep into setting goals, I would like to set the expectation for this chapter. The purpose here is for you to understand what marketing plans are, how to set them and how to achieve them. We are going to start with talking about the end goal: the destination and then we are going to work our way back to where we are now.

The very first thing to think of when setting goals (business or professional) is that they should be S.M.A.R.T. goals.

<u>S.M.A.R.T goals are a acronym for:</u>

S - Specific

M - Measurable

A - Attainable

R - Rewarding

T - Time Bound

Specific

A specific goal should be clear and easy to describe to someone else. It has to be crystal clear and have no fuzzy answers around it at all.

Measurable

It must be quantifiable to know whether you've attained them or not. A bad example of this is, *"I want to be rich"* because that's not measurable. But a goal like I want to make one hundred thousand-dollars by the end of this year is a great one because it's absolutely measurable.

Attainable

Make sure your goals are realistic so that you can know how to work towards achieving them. Don't set goals that are too difficult or impossible to achieve.

Rewarding

Make sure that the bar is set high up so that you can achieve them and when you achieve them, it excites you.

Time Bound

A goal without a time constraint is simply a wish. You have to create a sense of urgency and a time frame when you would like to get things done so that you can apply the necessary pressure to get it done.

Another thing you need to have in mind when setting goals is the symbolic meaning of the achievement of reaching that goal. Be clear as to what it *really* means to you when you achieve that goal. Ask yourself the "why" question long enough and you should find the answer you're looking for. An example:

Q: Why do I need the one hundred thousand-dollars?

A: It will get me a new car or other superficial items.

Q: Why do I need these items?

A: To feel better about myself.

Q: Why do I need to feel better about myself?

A: So that I can be more confident in life.

As you can see, you don't need $100k to be confident. Maybe in order to be confident you can set an easier goal to achieve; like lose 10 pds and get a 6 pack, or speak confidently in front of 50 people in the public arena (both of these was actually some of my personal goals at one point)

If you start really discovering the purpose of the goal by asking yourself "why?" enough times, I think you would discover what you are really trying to pursue may not need such a difficult goal.

Let's use the example of setting a much different goal: a goal of spending 2 weeks all expenses paid trip with my mother (allocating an exact budget amount) in Hawaii so we can deepen our relationship while participating in the volcano excursion she has wanted to see since a child.

Now, in the case of one hundred thousand-dollars, if I obtain one hundred thousand-dollars by the end of the year that will allow me to not only meet my financial goal, but also obtain another goal I have: spend two weeks with mom without worrying about anything but strengthening our relationship.

Really, the question is what's the life vision that you have when you are setting these goals? If your life vision is just to have a lot of money, that's not a vision, that's a financial goal, which you feel can get you somewhere you believe you want to be. It's really not connecting on a deeper level.

One of the other goals I would like to use as an example is my very big, hairy, audacious goal (also known by some as their bhaug) By the time I turn 40, I want to fly to the moon. The reason why I want to fly to the moon is not because I just think it's going to be cool; there's a deeper purpose behind it. It's because every quarter, I want to fly to a different destination and it's not going to be just any beautiful place on earth I want to go to, it's going to have a deeper meaning.

Every time I go there, it's going to have a deeper purpose; engaging with very specific people at every location.

The plan is to help those very specific humanitarians that are trying to do something to better their communities. In every one of these locations, I'm going to be contributing something to a social and community development. And after enough locations, I would have finally earned the right to fly to the moon.

So that is one of the examples I want to use about goal setting: Have the financial goal, have the relationship goal, have the career goal, have all kinds of goals. But attempt to have the BHAUG goal as well and try to integrate all the other goals into that one singular spearhead, that once achieved will solidify you have done an amazing thing with your life. You have achieved your ultimate goal: you have arrived at the possibility of obtaining your deeper purpose in life. (Yes, I know. Totally getting off the subject of how you can exponentially grow your real estate career right? Well stick with me, your almost there. Believe me, whether you use this for your specific real estate goals, or for life in general, this is good stuff.)

There are four questions I want to share with you after setting your goals that is like a sniff test to make sure they will work. They are really important to ask yourself and I don't know a lot of people that really ask these questions when they are setting goals except the person who shared them with me- John Butcher.

Before you start working towards the newly developed goals, you need to ask these questions to be sure when you meet those goals they are self-fulfilling and have a deeper purpose.

1. - Am I asking enough from myself?

Would you be proudly fulfilled when you accomplish these goals? I think if I fly to the moon that symbolizes a lot.

Jumping on a rocket and flying to the moon is of course awesome in itself but the steps it would take before I get to that point, that's something I'm going to be very fulfilled about.

2. - Are they achievable?

Can these things be done or is it worth striving towards?

3. - Am I willing to pay the price?

Think about this, anytime you make a goal, you're putting effort into it. You're probably taking effort out of something else.

You take out of one thing and put it into something else. If you make a financial goal for instance, you must know that it takes many hours of your time to make the financial goal. What do you have to sacrifice in other aspects of your life? It's the opportunity cost. You must ask yourself if you are willing to do whatever it takes to achieve that goal including at times sacrificing the ability to achieve other goals and most importantly- you may be sacrificing relationships.

4. - Will it truly make you happy?

You've got to have happiness in the journey and not just the destination. If all you're striving for is to get to the destination, what's going to happen when you get there? Are you going to be happy if you die just right after you get to that destination? Are you just going to set another destination and hope that you get there as well?

I think these four questions would sum up your goal setting and ensure that you are setting good goals and not just goals that would look good enough on paper. They are goals that make a difference and mean something to you on a deeper level.

We've talked about how to set general goals; important goals for your life in general. Now, we should look at goals specific to the sales strategies in real estate.

You could set specific goals like "I want to talk to ten leads per day or twenty leads per day" or "I want to attend 2 broker opens per week "and strategic goals such as" I'm going to not just have coffee every day with a different person but with someone that can connect me with my ideal avatar"

What are some of the ideas that you have for those specific day to day goals?

As an entrepreneur, you have to know how to be self-motivating. One problem entrepreneurs have is they wake up in the morning and they don't know what they really want to do, how many people to call, what hours to work, what tasks have to be done no matter what, etc. We are all victims of this! Life is always throwing curve-balls, especially when we're doing this on our own. But we need to become much clearer as to what actions is in-line with our yearly, quarterly, monthly, weekly and daily goals and what are not. It's as simple as this: everything that is *not* directly correlated with your goals comes second or even third.

For instance, your goal is to net ten-thousand-dollars profit a month from real estate. How many times contacting clients on average does it take to get a deal that will generate 10k? I know, I know…your answer is something like: "well Jeb, it really depends…blah blah" I'm not looking for that answer. Tell me a number, otherwise were going nowhere. Let's be brutal and say it takes you 200 points of contact with clients to get a deal that will generate 10k. Ok, now we have the goal in mind, we can work backwards to come up with a plan.

Now we can start to figure out how many calls do I need to make, how many meetings I need to attend, how many coffee dates I need to have. This is also a great way of measuring because you can find out what's working or not. If phone calls don't get you as good of results as personal meetings, then maybe schedule more face-to-face meetings. It ultimately is something you have to keep in mind as your business grows: where is my time best spent? And keep in mind this answer should really come from when you ask yourself: what is the things I'm doing in my business that has the highest effort-to-return ration? Meaning, identify what actions yield the biggest results. If you can find the efforts of one action take less energy, but yield the same results as another action that takes much more energy, then the answer should be clear: drop the action that takes more energy like a bad habit.

The only way you are going to discover this is by trial and observance. Anytime you make a call, you need to record it. How many calls did you have to make to get a warm lead? How many warm leads did it take to turn into a face-to-face interview; how many face-to-face interviews did it take to turn into a pre-qualification, and so on…

Breaking your business down like that gives you daily goals because when you wake up in the morning you can say "I have to visit five homes, engage with twenty people and then I have to make ten phone calls" Talk about direction- this gives you a reason to wake up in the morning; That's a solid and very specific daily goal.

I would put it simply; write down every way you can think of to get leads and try each one of them and remember to keep track of every one of them as well. If it's talking to the mail man, you've got to write down *"I talked to the mail man today"* and keep track of your results. Maybe it's a spreadsheet that you have all the "lead sources" listed and you simply put a check next to the column entitled mailman. However, you do it, track it! This shows how you how to identify your effort to return ratio so you can see what activates yield the best results.

After ninety -days, you're going to discover which of the methods produces more results than the others.

This is what I encourage you to observe;

    a) Which methods are getting more leads than the others?

    b) Think of something no one else is doing. Everyone is doing marketing and social media. Think about talking to the trash collector.

Once you've determined which contacts are getting the most leads, start thinking of how many contacts you had to make with that individual to turn into a lead and just set up your day so you know you need to make eight contacts today in order to turn a lead. And more importantly, you know it takes "X" leads to a close deal in order to accomplish your goals for the month.

You need to set out not just the big picture goals but the daily specific goals to help you accomplish your business goals. Now that we have our goals, lets figure out who we are going to market to.

Target Your Market

Find Your Avatar

This is called an avatar assignment and it is a one-page document my friend Henry created that allows you to discover *who* your ideal client is, not what farm area they are in. Realtors always are thinking about the farm area, but they really need to know who their client is before they begin marketing to them, regardless of the area, market or any number of other things. Every realtor should have the avatar questionnaire they can download, print and even hand out to others if need be.

Everyone should have one to three, maybe up to five avatars. That way, you are not just looking at everyone and hoping that something comes from it. You are looking for a very specific client and know exactly how to market to that client.

In this avatar assignment, you are going to be asked questions like;

- Who am I really after? Is it middle income Caucasian families that are looking to downsize? Is it an older gentleman that is selling a home his wife is tired of?

This assignment is going to help you determine and understand how to market to them.

What the Avatar Assignment will show you

I'm going to use an example of a conversation I just had with an agent.

I asked *"What is your avatar? "*

And he said *"What? "*

Then I said "Who are you targeting?"

He said *"Middle income "*

And then I said *"What do you mean middle income, can you be more specific? "*

Then he said *"Well, I'm looking for middle income Caucasian families "*

I said, *"Okay, where are you looking for these people? Where is your farm? "* *You have to narrow it down to a specific zip code "*

You need to find out who your ideal client is, how much money they make, and where they live. Think about where they are going to be, what they are going to do in their day-to-day lives and where you can interact with them.

This is how the avatar assignment helps you; it helps you find out what they do, what kind of books they read, what they do for fun on the weekends, and where they go to hangout on Friday nights.

All these questions help you get into the minds of your avatar in a way that says; if I was a "X", where would I be and what would I be doing? The obvious question here is: why would I go through this trouble Jeb? And here is the answer: Because you're going to figure out how to market like a genius like this and be way more effective than your competition!

An example of the avatar assignment at work

I had a conversation with a realtor that had filled out the avatar assignment. By filling out the questionnaire, the realtor was able to identify the ideal client was a husband and wife that needed to buy a smaller home because the teenagers in the home were graduating high school and moving away for college.

What's interesting is that high schoolers graduate right around the month of May and when looking at the calendar, guess what was going on last May? At the local theatre, they had the newest chick flick movie of a series come out so I said: "*Okay, think about this, your daughter is about to move off to college, you're really looking for an opportunity to spend some valuable time with them and you don't really know how much more time you're going to live with them when they move, so you want to do something that's interesting with them and spend some quality time together."*

What if you took her to the movies (because that's something she's interested in) and you're watching the opening credits and you have an advertisement that comes up that's specific to what's happening in your life. The advertisement reads along the lines of *"Looking to downsize, have a recently graduated student move to college? Need a smaller home? We're here to help you in any way that we can."*

And then it's got the name of your brokerage or better yet it's your recorded elevator pitch. So that's just one example that had played out with this gentleman because we identified who his avatar was, where we would be able to market in a way that was specific to his clients without wasting a lot of marketing dollars. (BTW- at the time I finished this book, he reported the new clients yielded from this strategy were by far the best he had seen in his business marketing when looking at his effort-to-return ratio.)

Why it's important to fill out the questionnaire

The task is to find your avatar- write down everything about that person that is going to be your target market:

Things you can write down include zip code, how old they are, what their educational level is, where do they work, and how much money do they make.

Try to describe their home- how many square feet, how many rooms, do they have a pool, what they do in their home for entertainment, do they have a lot of friends over, and how many kids do they have.

Also write down more about the kids; where do the kids go to school, do the kids go to college/high school, how old are their kids, do they go to private schools or public schools, what's their relationship with their kids, are they going to go away for college, are they going to move out or stay, are they going to come back after college, what are they doing nowadays, what's a life event they had/something that changed their life, what kind of magazine do they read, what type of books do they read, movies they go see, where do they like to go out maybe for dinner, the theatre, concerts?

What kind of car do they drive, why are they moving (this is one of the most important questions) are they moving up or down- downsizing or upsizing, maybe they have a pair of triplets or twins or the kids are going away to college, maybe they have six bedrooms in the house that they don't need any more? That's a perfect reason for downsizing.

When you describe your avatar, you're going to become your avatar, which is kind of cool because you have to think like that person and become like them to understand them.

If you become the avatar, you know how to market to the avatar. You would know how to write a letter to them, how to speak to them, how to push their hot buttons, and how to be sympathetic to them, knowing what their fears are.

All these things are important to know. These are the ways that you make a connection with such people. It's not about handing out a flyer that says *"Call me, local realtor."* ' It's connecting with them on a deeper level because you know what they're thinking.

What we are talking about is that you should be the contrarian; don't do what everyone else is doing. Do something different by getting into the mind of the person whom you are marketing to and becoming that person.

You should ensure that you always do something out of the ordinary. You can be a contrarian in a lot of ways but knowing your avatar is going to make you a marketing expert. Every agent should know that having an avatar is one of the requirements of a marketing expert.

When you hire a Vice President of Marketing for your real estate agency, you would be asked to show your avatar. Hence, having an avatar is using a strategy your competitors do not have because they cannot afford a marketing vice president or a chief marketing officer whom they have to pay about two hundred and fifty thousand to tell them what you already know now which is 'Have an Avatar.' By doing this, you just saved yourself two hundred and fifty thousand!

Go straight to the Source of Honey

Once you have identified where your ideal honey bee (client) is, go straight to the hive (source), and don't wait for it to come to you. The typical way is to find them individually but you can also find them collectively, just like getting honey from the source.

What I mean by this is you should try to find a location where these individuals meet on a regular basis. For example, let's say your ideal avatar is a real estate investor;

you know real estate investors do a lot of transactions; wouldn't that be great if you could track down somewhere where all the investors gather collectively?

For example, you can find out where real estate investors meet up in every city on a regular basis. You go to these locations where you see over a hundred and fifty investors in one room; that's a great opportunity to talk to a whopping one hundred and fifty potential clients all in one room.

And one thing that is really interesting about real estate investors' meetings is that at the beginning of the meetings, they give anyone who is willing, a thirty second opportunity to go up there and make a pitch and I always say, "Why don't real estate agents go there to pitch?" That could be you up there, pitching to the real estate investors.

What if you went out there and with every meeting you have a purpose; like in this example, your purpose is to find investors:

"My name is Jeb Durgin, I've been sent here by God to save you all from having to deal with crappy agents who don't know how to work hard and are not willing to be teachable. Instead of giving you a business card at the end of today's meeting that somewhere on it says, 'The best

compliment is a referral', I'm going to tell you that the biggest compliment is giving me fifteen minutes of your time. And while you're drinking the cup of coffee I just bought for you that it takes to fill those 15 minutes, I'll show you five surefire ways to help your business make more money immediately. No need to try and write down my phone number, just remember I'm the guy with the green bowtie, (or whatever your wearing to stand out in a crowd) or simply go to the back of the room and look for the red blinking light on the table with all my contact information. You can't miss it"

What's interesting about this is when you go to these investor meetings, at the back, there's usually all these papers set out. They all look exactly the same but what I've done in this speech is;

1 - Hopefully, I'm making a speech so impactful that people are all over me after I'm done that I don't have the time to talk to everyone but;

2 - I've also let them know that if I'm not available, you could still get my contact information on the table and it's going to stand out because it's going to be the one with the red blinking light!

It's totally opposite from everyone else's. I don't care how many other papers are out there, the one with the red blinking light is pretty obvious so if you don't get a chance to talk to me because I'm so busy with other investors, you can grab my contact.

You should also make sure that on your business card it says *'Real Estate Consultant'* not *'Real Estate Agent.'*

Think about how much more powerful a consultant is and you can even take it a step further and put a fish bowl that says *"Don't call me, I'll call you, drop your card or phone number here"* And put a notepad so that if they don't have a card, they can drop their numbers. You can be different that way because you would have to call them back.

Then you can do a follow up the next month and say in the last thirty days, you've sold two homes for people that you met there at the investors meet up or you can say your value proposition such as *"My Husband is an interior designer and for every house I sell, I would furnish it fully"* or whatever your value proposition is that no one else can do but you.

Set up a Filter Process

What's interesting about this is that you can say now I've got one hundred and fifty real estate investors calling me but I don't want to deal with one hundred and fifty real estate investors calling me. So you would set up a filter process; by having some very easy questions for them when they call you so that you can quickly determine whether they are serious clients or not.

After the qualifying phase, you can move to the next phase, which is to categorize them. Decide what each investor wants; some investors just want to deal with land opportunities, some others want to deal with multi-million dollar homes, so what you do here is filter out the ones you don't want to deal with and categorize them not only under the type of investors they are, but what kind of bargains they are looking for.

You don't have to pass clients over, even if you don't have what they want at the moment. You can keep their contacts so that the next time you get what they want, you'll know who to call.

Consider the Lifetime Value of Each Client

You also need to know the lifetime value of your customer because you could be a full-time investor and all you do is buy and hold; that's not as valuable to me as an investor who buys and flips because we're talking of multiple transactions in one year with the same property.

A flipper may go through two homes a month, both buying and selling. Then the other full time investor that buys and holds may buy two homes a month, but he's not selling.

If you have exclusivity with a couple of investors and they each do two homes per week, you're going to blow it out of the water. As an agent, you may think that investors take too much of your time but think about it, you have ten offers before one of them gets accepted and it took you a lot of time (5 hours total?) to write those offers well. Compare that to a typical buyer who you had to show at least a couple of houses (easily five hours with paperwork) before they bought. Think about it; is it the same amount of time?

Now that you've got them to buy the home, and that you know you are closing the deal, what's the probability that the first time homeowner is going to sell in the next 90-days? But that's more likely for the home flipper. So you have to think about where you want to put your efforts at; the one that'll make you the most money would be my plan.

Another thing to think about is the referrals. How nice would it be if your ideal avatar not only did two transactions a year, but also gave you referrals?

So let's say a real estate investor does one transaction a month of five thousand-dollars, that's sixty thousand-dollars a year. Then you need to think about how much you are willing to spend to connect with that client. The lifetime value of that client might be two hundred thousand but a typical homebuyer's lifetime value might be fifteen thousand-dollars; they bought a house and referred another client but you're going to spend more money reacquiring clients compared to a real estate investor who you can acquire just once.

In conclusion to avatars: You as an agent need to decide where you want to spend your time and what kind of clients are good for you. I think the avatar assignment is a really good way to figure out what kind of person you're really looking for and secondly, what's the source where you can meet them collectively because if you go to the source, it's going to be much easier to meet them then trying to pick them off one by one. Let's think of other ways we can generate new business.

How to Get New Business

84 Ways to Find a Lead

Everyone wants leads and I have all kinds of ideas for how to find them.

I'm going to share the eighty-four ways that I've collected with you guys through a link, email, webpage or something, don't worry…I'll make sure you get the list! But better yet, not just eighty-four ways that I've thought of to find a lead, but more importantly, a way for you to figure out what Leads are most worth pursuing. This is added material you will find either at the end of the book, or on my website. Here are just a few of the examples I pulled from that material:

Networking in Real Estate Selling –

Networking is one of the things that real estate professionals are good at and at the same time bad at. They think they are networking smartly but in the real sense, they don't do it right. Networking can yield good results if applied properly.

But how do you network together with others? How can you create and expand your circle of influence?

Let's use an example of a Realtor that has about thirty customers and is expecting referrals from those customers and other professionals. In order to enact the law of reciprocity, the question should be: How can the Realtor first give referrals to those customers and professionals? That customer may be website developer, a food and beverage sales reap, or they may be an electrician, a carpet cleaner, a plumber, or a handyman the idea here is to find out in which ways I can help grow the success of my customers and other professionals before my own. By doing this, you will be amazed how much business makes its way back to you. ADD VALUE

The average real estate agent is constantly asking for a hand out, not adding value. A very common example of this typical hand out is the postcard you likely receive on your door step or in the mail. This postcard has a picture of the Realtor, a large one, and it doesn't show or say anything about real estate or the product. Basically, it is the same story of about "me."

In one of my conversations with a top selling agent, he said none of the postcards he sends even have his picture on it. He knows that he is not selling himself but the house. He wants to pass the message that, "It's not about my handsome face or about me but about you the customer and your house that matters most." The fact of the matter is, if you are good at what you do, once you meet the client face to face, its game over anyways. There is no need to talk about anything other then what the client wants.

What a real estate agent needs to do is turn the tables around and instead of saying, "I'm looking for more clients and instead say:, "I'm looking for real estate related problems" So, this seems innately opposite of what you would want to hear right? Well guess what: we are all about doing things exactly opposite to what others are doing! You see, it's not about handouts. It's about showing your expertise and earning the business by finding a solution to their problem. And believe me; you're in a much better position having fixed problems for someone then asking them how they can fix yours.

Let's use an example of the client asking for help with a terrible leak that had just happened the night before. They managed to get the water off, but need help fixing it. the Realtor can tell a plumber from his contacts about the situation, and will likely receive a referral fee from the plumber, and before the plumber goes to the property for the repair, simply let him know you pay a one-thousand-dollar referral fee for any property you can list because of he suggested using you as a real estate agent.

Now, the Realtor here is in a way better position for getting a commission. He just solved problems for multiple people. I don't know about you, but I'm much more likely feel comfortable with someone that has done something for me, especially solve one of my problems.

In such a case, all three parties in the network will benefit. The homeowner benefits because the plumber is able to help them fix the immediate problem of a leak. If the plumber refers you to the homeowners as an agent that can either help them find a new house or sell this house you obviously benefit. The plumber not only benefits from the having the job, but is also benefiting in that they will be paid for the referral they get. The Realtor ultimately gets the most because he or she has proven that they are the go-to resource when it comes to anything real estate related... It may not happen immediately, but guess what: the more solutions you have for their problems, the more they will trust you, like you and want to keep coming back to you for business, including selling or buying a home.

It's important the agent can educate the plumbers, electricians, handymen and gardeners on how they can take advantage of a situation before they go on the call. This includes educating these professionals on how they can approach the homeowner when they're doing the repair or cleanup, and be able to connect them to the Realtor.

One great advantage of a Realtor taking the role of an educator is that he or she takes out the fear homeowners or home buyers have with Realtors. Homeowners think of Realtors as sales people.

But when a Realtor takes a different approach of offering solutions to problems by educating the home owners, it creates a positive image and not that of a typical salesman. This way, the Realtor can win the confidence of the home buyers. An agent therefore can act as a consultant. Educating the home buyers makes them feel that they are not being forced into situations or circumstances, but they are in control of the decision they make since they are offered options to consider. And this is the beauty of consulting or educating others by real estate agents.

Business Cards –

It's most likely that you have a stack of business from networking events, open house events, business meetings and a number of other places. You may already have a strategy for organizing these cards: maybe you place them in a stack organized by what event you met them at. Maybe you organize based on what their profession is. Whatever the case, you're stuck with a crap-load of business cards your toting around. Let's get with the age of technology my people. There are many apps that allow you to do all this organizing on the digital cloud. You take photos of the business cards and place them in your online contacts. These may be your phone contacts, iPhone contacts, Gmail contacts, or many other contact locations

Remember, just because you have that contact in your list, it doesn't mean you will remember to follow up. It means if they called you on your phone or emailed you, you will recognize know who they are. That's very important because you can even respond by asking what they have done since you have seen them at last month's event downtown. That in itself shows you know the people whom you have exchanged contacts with even if you didn't talk since then.

Now, this is what I suggest you do;

1. Get Gmail. Best thing in the world for integrating everything.

2. Download your Gmail account onto your phone

3. Use the camera on your phone. It will link to your Google or Gmail account- every time you take a photo of the details of a business card, you can send that information straight to your Gmail contacts

4. Create a Google+ account where the contacts are also uploaded

5. Link your social media accounts with your Google account.

Whenever you take the photo of business card and the information is uploaded to the contacts lists, the people are automatically invited to join your Google+, Twitter and LinkedIn networks.

Every time they do a search about a topic or keyword about real estate such as 'San Diego home', you pop up number #1 on the search results. Remember, all of this is a backup if you forget to add them in your newsletter list, so it's like free marketing! And it's a hell of lot easier then carrying around a stack of business cards in an oversized rolodex.

One other thing about business cards: How many times have you seen the same vista print card with a different name on it? It's the same exact graphics, font, size and finish as the last one you received? BORING.

You need to differentiate yourself from the rest. Have something out of the ordinary. You can find business cards made of wood, metal, plastic, 3D versions, or even a bi-fold business card.

For example, there is one that is bi-fold, when you open it up; it has an image that pops up. I found an option of getting a business card where when you open it, it takes the

shape of a house! What this means is that you can have a
3D print of a house— and on it, you can have contact info
printed. So, when you hand someone that business card, not
only is it not like every other card they receive, but it is
something they make a comment about: this thing is
awesome!

I know what you're thinking: that thing probably costs $3 a
card!! Jeb, my vista-print card only costs .20 cents each.
But let's think about this for a moment: you go home after
an event with a stack of cards, all of them exactly the same
as every other card you have received except there was one
that folds out like a house! If I'm efficient, all of the cards
are going in my database, and then I throw them in the
trash. EXCEPT the one that folds out like a house. That one
is going on my desk.

Every day, your name is in front of that person. Every time
they sit down at their desk, they are subconsciously
thinking about you. They may not even recognize your
name until someone asks for a realtor and they say,
"Actually I totally know a guy! If he is anything like his
business card, he probably thinks outside the box to get
things done." Was that not the cheapest and most effective
marketing you have ever done? Was it worth 3$ to have
your name in front of that person every single day for
stinking eternity? You bet your butt it was.

And you can even get even more creative and design your business card to be in form of a fold out knife (look it up. There are business cards that fold out to be real knifes!) or something else practical people may always keep in their wallet. This is something that people are going to be seeing every day and not just going to put it on their home cupboard drawers or workstation cabinets. It has to be something cool that people would love carrying with them every time or placing on their desk and showing everybody that comes in.

What about placing your contact info on a key-shaped USB they can keep on their key-ring? And on that flash disk, you can have information about you, the short video that says who you are, your 30-second pitch and outlines the referral program. The possibilities are endless; you can just think of anything that can be made as a business card. That is part of your business plan and branding. These are things that you can incorporate in your business plan so that you get away from doing the typical to doing things differently.

Door Knocking–

Another example that I've thought of which is also about being a contrarian is, after determining who your avatar is, go door knocking while wearing a uniform with a logo. YES, I know it sucks. Stick with me for a second.

I've done research in the past about this and I've discovered that you get three times as much response when you wear a uniform that says what company you belong to.

People are not threatened and they know you're a reliable estate agent. You could wear a suit but just make sure you accessorize with something that carries a logo and says something about who you are and what you represent.

One good thing about having an avatar is that it would show you the type of person they would be comfortable with you showing up at the door. You can test this by dressing in different ways on different days; one day jeans and polo, the next day, a suit and a tie then you observe their body language and their reactions to see who they feel more comfortable with.

The next thing you want to do is to make sure you have a script. You could deviate from your script but having a baseline script is good to give a direction of where the conversation should go and to also serve as a measure to determine how the conversation is working and if you're going in the right direction.

Another trick for door knocking is when you go and park in that neighborhood, hopefully you have a branded vehicle; you could put a sign that says "I will be here all week."

You could put your photo so that when people open the door or sneak to see who it is, they'll say, "Oh, it's the guy that's going to be here all week."

So now they're expecting and they are not afraid to open the door, and if it's a branded vehicle, or a car with your logo or even a magnetic sign, it should say, "I will be here all week." This way they know that if they don't get you on Monday, they're going to get you on Tuesday, on Wednesday, or they could even go to your car and leave their phone number there if they need to speak with you. You could also leave them a note that says you are going to be around all week and they could give you a call or book an appointment.

One of the secrets I learned from Toastmasters (a public speaking development course) is when you have the script, it's good to test how powerful the script is by recording it on your phone and first watch the video to see if your body language portrays the message you are trying to pass across. Then secondly, put your headphones in and listen to it without the video to see if your voice reflects the message as well. This would help you figure out ways to improve on your script.

It's important to know what you look like when speaking your script because it helps to build your confidence and makes you more comfortable.

Also, you need to sound natural when delivering your script; it can't be word for word. Whether you're networking, drinking coffee or presenting a home, you need to record a video, practice everything from your greeting, to the actual speech and the farewell speech.

Also, whenever you are speaking to a potential client, think of the objections they may have as they come up. You already have your avatar so it's easy for you to figure out some of the questions they may have and decide on how to answer them. If you already have answers to those objections, when they come up, they won't come up as a surprise.

You could think about some of the fears of that individual or what keeps them up at night. These are their fears and you can educate them about how to get out of such situations.

You don't just go knocking on their doors asking them for business or asking them to make you more money, but you could open a dialogue with them, show them you are interested in their needs and in connecting with them on a deeper level.

Remember also to always give value before you ask for business. If you did your research before, when they open the door you might tell them, I want to be the realtor for this neighborhood, here is the research that I've done on your house and then you hand them a value package; a package that contains valuable information about their home, market trends in that zip code, what may influence the value of their home and the benefits they can get from selling.

Also, you should do your research before you go knocking on doors so you can know if they are the owners of the home or just renting! How much time and money are you wasting on marketing to properties that are not even occupied by the person who has the ability to sell? Always make sure to ask for their email addresses and phone numbers.

Deciding when to ask questions and when to deliver those conversations is also very important because the reality is they've heard it all already. Like if you say "I'm a top performer" you also must keep in mind it could mean different things to different people. It could actually mean something negative. It's indirectly telling them you will likely be dealing with my team, not me directly.

Also, when you are talking to the homeowner, make sure to incorporate value in education; you're helping them to learn about the process. You may not get a chance to sell to them today but you would have already planted a seed and connected with them on a level that no one else has done before so the next time they see you, they may say "I'm still not interested in selling my home but guess what, you impacted me in such a way that I had a conversation with my niece and she is interested"

Door knocking when hosting a house warming party:

Everybody hates door-to-door sales. It irritates people to hear the door knocked on. But with something like house warming party, it is a different thing. You are not bothering anybody, your inviting them to a party. After they come to the party and see how you are the awesome realtor we all wished we had, you have the opportunity to grow your business ten times.

It's pretty simple, make a point of visiting the neighborhood, and ask them to join their new neighbor who just joined their community. You are not selling; you are hosting a house warming party for your client. Tell the neighbors, "You don't have to bring anything— we already have food drinks, gifts, music and more." At the party these people will definitely ask you, "Who are you?" At that time, you are grabbing their attention. They want to know more about you. Right then, you may not know it, but you're selling yourself in an atypical way. There is no cold calling, no door knocking in a position of weakness. It's different here; you are doing your selling on position of friendliness, comradery and strength. If you meet twenty or thirty neighbors in one day— that means you may have at least twenty new hot leads in one day. If you spend an hour with these people in the party, you have a great opportunity at your hands.

So you open up doors that you may not even be aware of. It's not that you didn't get to sell today; it's that you're planting a seed for tomorrow. You need to understand that this isn't about the hard sell; it's about making a deeper connection with them and being recognized. Getting a chance to connect with them in a way that other people can't.

Use the circle of other professionals to find leads–

Now, this circle of professionals can be used in many ways. This truly is a powerful list of people. Let's think about how else we can use this list. What if this list of people could get you additional business? What If each one of these professionals gets you an additional one or two home buyers or sellers? This alone could double your business.

Remember, these are people who move from house to house making repairs and installations. During their visits, they may overhear the owners of a home say something like "I'm so sick of this roof problem or plumbing problem…we really need to get a new home". That should ring like a bell to the person listening. That carpenter or insulation guy should be recommending that desperate homeowner to consider visiting you, the Realtor, to help them find a new home to buy. If nothing else, they should have taken down the client's name and phone number and shared it with you. Why? For one, you have helped grow his business, and he now has the chance to grow yours. This is called the law of reciprocity. It works very simply; it basically states if you do something for me, I'll do something for you. He now has the chance to grow yours. And guess what, if they buy another house with you, it likely will have problems in the future that will need a carpenter. Who will they call for that work to be done? Well at this point it should be obvious.

Do Realtors ever consider this as another option to grow their business? Again, probably not. You may be familiar with this tactic through certain business networking groups, but the reality is I hardly (like only one time) see realtors using this.

The carpenters, carpet cleaners, masonry guys, appliance repair guys, HVAC technicians, and many others can be part of the business circle. All of these guys can refer clients to you.

You can print the directory of the professionals you consider the "circle of power" and give it to these same individuals or professionals who are on the directory and they can give it out to the owners of homes they come into contact with. This way, you are reaching out to hundreds of homeowners and now everyone grows their business together.

If you have ten people in the circle of power and you give them the print out of the directory, they will more than likely reach out to many more people. For example, if it is a plumber and he has one hundred clients a year, you will have one hundred people who begin to trust you because they have been recommended by a person who they trust. Your network has extended to a hundred homes, if not a thousand!

When you receive a call from someone or a home buyer who has been referred by a plumber in your circle of power, you want to ensure you give them greater attention and offer incentives. You want to offer premium service to that prospective client. The circle of power is like a private club. The people referred will get a free inspection; a twenty percent discount; your cell phone number; and, you can mention them all when talking. Make sure your offer is for superior service at very affordable prices. Consider giving the client surprises something special when they call you for a quote.

From all these efforts, you have someone that is interested in using your services. They reach out to you with an urgent message. They seem to be a hot lead. What next?

Qualifying the Lead

After going through the process and you've discovered you've got a lead, someone has just given you their number saying "Oh, I want to sell my house," you have to qualify the lead. Qualifying the lead in this case means knowing the appropriate person who would buy the house your about to list.

The first thing you must know is what kind of condition the house is in. Is it retail ready? This is called retail because it is turnkey and the home is ready to be sold as is, it has just been recently built or recently remodeled and in perfect condition. Suitable buyers for this might be first time home owners because they don't want to do so much work, they just want to buy a house, move into it and live there for the next twenty years.

The second option is the light rehab (aka pre-hab) home. What this means is the home needs just a little bit of renovation. Maybe it just needs paint and carpet. This might be a perfect home for rental property or a quick flip back on the market.

The third category is the full rehab. In this case, you've got this guy who wants to sell the home but the home is in a bad condition; there are holes in the floor and rats everywhere. This is a perfect home for a rehabber.

Qualifying the lead is not just about determining whether you're going to take the client or not, it's about knowing your exit strategy. It helps you know who your potential buyer is because if you know who your buyer is, you're going to spend a lot less time, money and effort on marketing. If you've done extensive networking, you're going to already have a list of people who would be interested in each one of these possible situations; the couple that wants the perfect home, the gal who needs a home that she can buy and rent out, or the dude that wants to fix and flip.

Lastly, you need to know where the war zone is. These are areas where we stay away from. For instance, places you're scared to drive at night, the ghettos, places that you know are gang territory and would rather avoid.

At the end of the day, this is where you say: "This is not an area I currently do business in, but I appreciate you reaching out to me. I have someone I trust that I would like to put you in contact with. They know this area very well." This is also where your networking comes in because now you can send this to somebody who loves this neighborhood, someone who loves this niche. Now you can provide value to another agent.

There are also a couple of sources that you can tap into that can tell you what kind of location that a house is in. There's actually a really cool application that my friend John Cochran created. It's called a 'sweet spot locator' and it basically breaks down which zip codes or which areas are pre-hab zones, rehab, and war zones and gives you statistics as to why they are what they are, and helps you figure out which ones to stay away from and which ones to pursue.

Another free website I use often to help me learn how bad a neighborhood can be is called Crimemappers.com. The website shows you how many crimes have taken place in a designated area. You can filter all kinds of things like how far your parameter is on a map, (one block, one mile) what time frame you would like to review (one month, one year) what type of crime it was (petty theft, homicide) etc.

Quick Analysis

How great would it be if I knew I had a house that was a buy-and-hold property and I'm able to call the guy that wants a rental and once they are on the phone I tell them "here is the numbers you're going to want" If you've taken a step to find out who your ideal client is, you would know that some basic pro-forma is all you really need.

You can also show him multiple exit strategies. What I mean by this is maybe you show them what they could do if a certain exit strategy doesn't work, like how they can still make a profit from flipping the property out if they are unable rent it. These are just a couple of examples of adding value to your client and really spending the time to get to know their business. How much more valuable to you think it is to get this phone call "Hey, I got you the perfect property for you, this is the expected cash return and this is the ROI". Rather then: "I think I may have seen something that may work for you, but I don't really know" Just by taking that extra step, you would be able to prove you are a credible source and anytime you call them. You bet they're going to you over anyone else that calls with the latter script.

Regardless of which call I get; I'm going to be thankful. Why? Because I just got a lead. Maybe it's a cold lead, maybe it's a steaming hot-burning fire lead. The fact of the matter is, whatever it is, it's important to keep in mind we need to say thank you to those who thought of us when sending over the information. In this next section, we are going to be talking about how to create a referral program so we can do exactly that: thank others for the business they are sending our way.

Developing a Referral Program

When you want to develop your referral program, you need to get away from the typical marketing to something new. You need to use a "leads now money later" strategy.

As a Realtor, your typical marketing strategy is probably "money now leads later." This is what most real estate agents are doing. Realtors are paying money now and reaping the benefits later. They are paying for things like advertising in the hope that they will get business later. However, there is a better way and you only have to pay when you actually get leads! It is much more effective and will give waaaayy better results.

In the real estate business, there are many people who can help you generate business.

What you need to do is to create a detailed script both on print and on video to eliminate any confusion about how this referral program is going to work. You will need to post this everywhere including in your email signature.

You can say, "P.S. Want to make some additional money? Click here to find out more about my referral program." This should be something catchy and which will grab the attention and interest of people to consider working and relating with you.

Keep in mind that with the referral program, whatever you consider to give as compliment (it may be dinner, gifts, free services, or something else), it doesn't have to be cash. It really is only limited by your imagination.

You need to think like this: Anybody who recommends a customer to you is going to get something. You probably have recommended some business to other professionals and didn't get anything. It may have been a lawyer, an insurance rep, or a handyman you recommended but you likely received nothing in return from the referred business how much more would you be recommending that professional if they were giving you something in return for the referred business every time you set someone to them? You are different, and you appreciate others and you will show it! They will know and feel you value and recognize them for the business they bring to you, no matter how small

The referral program is not just meant for the realtors. All of the people you work with should be using it. What's really cool about this type of thanks is that everyone gets something out of the additional business. It's not just one party who is benefiting from this network, but all.

An everyday example

You attend one of those business networking events we have all been to and you meet ten people. As we all know, this is where business cards are handed out like candy at the bank. Sometimes you don't even want to take it, but the person insists you do. So you reluctantly take their business cards and think to yourself: I'll never call this guy. Well guess what, I don't care what they do, how experienced they are, or how much you don't think it's worth it, you follow up with them. In the follow up email, you say, "It's a pleasure to meet you at last night's event. I have attended a few of these events, and I want to be honest, I meet a lot of people that I never do business with. I want you to know it is my full intention we do business together. I'm thinking of you next time someone I know needs a "---" This, in itself, is a strong statement you send to them. You start by saying that you will give them a business. You may notice you have not started directly by asking for referrals from them but you said that you will send them business. ADD VALUE.

Oh and by the way, I have never had another professional s say they would not give some kind of kick-back if I sent them business. Why do we start by offering to send them business rather then ask for them to send you business? Let me tell you a secret—the best way to grow your business is to grow someone else's. As the great Zig Ziglar once said: You will get all you want in life if you help enough other people get what they want..."

On the email, you can continue and say, "Oh and by the way, it's without having to be said but obviously if you refer somebody to me, you will make money instantly. As in I drop a check in the mail the same day."

Now, you are saying you will not only send them referrals, but you also give them the opportunity to get something from you if they send you business. I love this way of saying it too, kind of like it was a fleeting thought that you actually wanted them to send you any kind of business. Plus, the little nugget about instant cash always appeals to anyone reading it. After saying that, you can tell them to click on the link to find out how they will make money. They will click on the link and go to view the video you have created about the referral program. From there, they will learn they can get things like dinners, gift cards, or cash for referring clients to you. It's all included in the Power Referral Package I will be talking about later in this book.

Creating a budget for a referral program

Budget to get new business

This is about getting new business from other professionals related to real estate. The gift doesn't have to be actual money, but you need to develop a dollar amount for this budget. What if you offer a thousand dollars as a referral fee paid to anyone that can send a lead on a client that closes escrow? One thousand for the first home, and two thousand-dollars for every other home lead they send thereafter? Most people will want to get the first transaction out of the way to quickly advance to the real money. When you do this, you will probably get at least two homes, no matter what happens, and that is twenty-thousand-dollars in commission and eight hundred-thousand-dollars in transactional value. (using the averages mentioned earlier in the book)

Maybe the budget will be ten percent for the first time deal and twenty percent of the transaction for the following deals-it's really up to you to decide. That's the whole idea of leads now, money later for marketing to get leads. This is not putting up fliers, door hangers, creating websites, and hand writing welcome to the neighborhood cards. It's getting closer to people who go out to give you this business, but in an influential way. These people only get paid when they when a property closes escrow. It's like you just hired these professionals to work for you. It's a zero risk program.

That's a budget a Realtor can afford... by allocating only ten percent of the commission you're getting paid, you can deliver an incredible gift that separates you from the crowd— not just the competition. This is something you want to do for every single person who gets your business.

Where your maintenance budget is best spent

We just discussed where to spend money on clients that send you business but this is for the clients who have sent you business in the past but have not recently? How do you keep connected with them? How many times are you going to call them in year? Are you going to send them newsletters? Will you invite them for coffee?

Remember the customers have not yet any new business. How do you maintain this budget?

Let's play with a budget of one thousand-dollars a year spent on your customers. The goal is to get five transactions from one customer. One thousand-dollars spent to make fifty-thousand-dollars dollars is nothing. But are you doing it?

The top performing agents may be sending newsletters—
but what I have seen is just some digital copies. Nobody is
doing print copies, which may be more enticing than the
digital copies.

A printed newsletter that goes out would be a great idea.
It's about one hundred -dollars a year, and this is fairly
small.

A tip for the agents: Printed newsletters are the best kept
secret in real estate marketing.

When you send out a newsletter, only twenty percent is
business, and 80 percent is personal. That's where you talk
about the experiences you had at ball games; the books you
have been reading; how your children did in school. It's
where you offer tips for parents of teenagers. You can talk
about your kid's exciting experiences. People want to know
you, so it's your story here. But this only takes one hundred
-dollars.

What about the nine hundred and fifty-dollars left out in the
budget of one thousand-dollars?

The remaining can be spent on things like a birthday gift of
about one hundred and fifty-dollars a year. The only happy
birthday gifts I have received from my agents have been on

Facebook and social media sites- you know, the ones that automatically send you a reminder to send the "happy birthday" message. They only wish me Happy birthday on these social sites, and they call that a gift. That's the kind of gifts I have received— nothing really.

How powerful would it be to see a Realtor show up on a customer's birthday with presents and gifts? The mere act of showing up on someone's birthday with gifts makes the difference. Realtors can buy some steaks for a barbecue; buy the cakes, best hamburgers, and any number of other items.

Make sure you know the interest of the customers and give them something that would make them happy and keep on remembering you. Think of buying something like a custom made incense burner or a pair of nice sunglasses. You may want to consider the value of the present or gift rather than the cost. Also think about how often they will be using the item, the more they use it, the more they will be thinking of you, consciously or not.

A bottle of wine made by a local winery and it is personalized— that can be another idea of a gift. The wine bottle can have the name printed on it. (And for heaven's sake- please don't leave a price tag on it)

A vase with fresh flowers and a name printed on it delivered on a birthday is also a practical idea. Find out what the kids of the clients like and offer that during their birthdays.

Perhaps you can get two nice bottles of wine, something for the house, gift certificate for special dinner, or anything that adds value to their special day. It could also be something that they can keep in the house.

How about a I bought my house today Anniversary gifts? It's a great way to celebrate when they bought their dream home— this also works great as a point of contact.

A customer doesn't want a Realtor to call them and ask for more business. The customer wants a Realtor who shows up and says, "Guess what! You didn't know this... today is your house-buying anniversary day and I got a present for both of you and for your lovely kids." The kids will begin to ask, "Who is this guy? He should be your best friend."

A two hundred-dollars allocation for this special day would be perfect. A candle lit dinner even makes things spicier. It helps to remember the day a client bought his house. It's one year, two or ever three years since the client bought the house. The client wants to remember the memories, and there is nothing better than having an anniversary dinner.

At the dinner, you can find out if there are any concerns the client has about the house. Does he need to update his homeowner's insurance? Are there leaking roofs or plumbing issues? Is the insulation working properly? The customer would probably need some help on something, and as a awesome Realtor, you definitely can offer some help. These are things you may learn about when you show up to the special dinner event.

If you do that two times for each kind of event or interaction in a year, you are keeping constantly in touch with the clients. This is a budget well spent.

What all this means is you have a point of contact during the birthdays anther special event dates. Offer them just what they appreciate. These are points of contact you are creating and not a call. You are interacting and relating with the client through these special events and they will always appreciate that.

Besides scheduled visits, as a Realtor, you also want to have impromptu visits. You just show up with an offer at least once a month to the home. When you show up, it's like you are the pride of the day. It's like when you have been away and the pet has missed you.

When you come in, you can see the kind of happiness and joy the pet has. You are now part of the family and you bring happiness to the family. When you are away, the family feels like they have a friend taken away from them. Because of maintaining this contact, you have become a longtime friend to your customer. The relationship with them has grown even bigger and your real estate selling business is making strides when others are closing down.

Don't just think that what you need to do is call your customers and ask them how they are doing. Make a point of making visits whether formalized or surprises. It all adds up to building social business that can outweigh the formal or the typical way of doing your real estate business.

REFERRAL PROGRAM MECHANICS:

In essence, you can develop many referral programs and types; you can do joint venture programs with other realtors and not just a referral program. Everybody needs to outline that in their business plan including;

a)   Are you going to have dinner, gift cards, free services, discounts, and the like?

b)   How much are you going to pay?

You should attach a budget to each of the programs we have talked about. For example, if the value of a customer is ten-thousand-dollars, are you going to spend five hundred -dollars or one thousand-dollars?

Some of the gifts we talked about are such as sending people to Disney Land or to Hawaii, but again, what is your allocation if the customer is valued ten-thousand-dollars? Is it one percent, five percent, twenty percent, or what?

Lastly, how you follow up or deliver the gift is immensely important. You do not need to do it casually; make sure it brings some emotional touch to the people you present by being there presently or delivering an emotionally catching email. And, you can take part in the actual time of the gift such as spending time together to have coffee with the person who send you a lead or join a family on a holiday vacation at Lake Tahoe.

POWER REFERRAL PACKAGE

What's the easiest way to go about this you ask? Create a "Referral Power Package" In this referral package you can highlight all the items that are important. It's a breakdown of how exactly the referral is paid, it's a signed contract stating you will in fact do it. (I typed mine on a word document and it's only a paragraph long. The fact of the matter is that most people don't care exactly how it's written or how long, if it's in writing and it's signed its all of a sudden real. Verbal agreements are one thing, but once it's on paper its totally different, even if it's a paragraph long) the package also includes handouts they can print out and leave behind. It highlights who the ideal clients are. It's a Cd with mock scenarios or actual interviews with past clients. These are real life examples of where they can have a conversation with others in the same way they always do, except they are able to recognize key indicators that show an awesome realtor may be exactly what someone is looking for.

In order to ensure you keep the referral program working optimally, you want to create different scripts for others to use so that when they come across your ideal avatar, (client) they know exactly what to say. This script would ideally be included in your 'power referral package". You can even help those in the referral program by providing them with a sample script, which they can modify to apply on their area of expertise or industry. Make sure you let them know they have to be flexible in words they use. And, most importantly, let them know that they should speak from their heart. Try to show them how the referral program works and how it can play out in their industry.

In summary, if an agent is going to have a productive networking group, they have to shift their approach in the real estate selling business. The agents need to offer opportunities to the people, professionals, or customers they engage with in a network to also benefit. Quit asking for a handout and start offering one. Literally: It's called the power referral package and it will make them lots of money and in return, make you even more.

It's about how "we can do more together."

HOW TO SAY THANK-YOU

I want to share something everyone knows but rarely uses: everyone loves a thoughtful gift. I challenge you to actually be present with the people you meet in your life. Genuinely be interested in what makes them tick, what made them happy, what kind of things they are into. It's a bit like courting a new boyfriend or girlfriend. Pick up on the things that make them truly happy. Maybe it's a cup of coffee at the same rink-a-drink coffee stand downtown. Now consider this; when they send you a lead, as a way of saying thank you to them, you ask if they will meet you at their favorite coffee stand so you can buy them a cup of Joe. When you meet, you order their drink and hand it to them with $100 gift card to the coffee stand. BOOM. They were not expecting that. It shows you care about them, what they enjoy in life and how something as small as a cup of coffee can make someone so happy.

What is most important here is not even the gift card but how you present it. It's really best if you can deliver the gift card in person with a hand written note that says, "I want to let you know I truly appreciate your lead and for you to be thinking of me; here is small token of my gratitude: a gift card for coffee, you and me." So you're not just giving them a gift card for coffee but you will also be there to have the coffee with them.

Again, the value of the compliment depends on the value of the lead. It can even be one dinner a month. You can even have another option, which is a point system where you reward points for every referral and more points when the lead becomes a client. So, the people referring you leads will get points, which they accumulate and they can redeem them after some time for something tangible.

It's also very important anytime anyone asks to learn about the referral program, you also say thank you. You should send them a $5 Starbucks card and Thank you card just for inquiring. This is just a small token of appreciation for showing their interest in the program. You are saying a small thank you— just by somebody raising their hand to say that they want to know more about the referral program.

If the person learns more about the program and sends a lead, you have to place them in your list. It can be in your newsletter or email blast— anything that gives them updates.

Okay, now let's jump forward. Let's pretend all this hard work has paid off and you finally have a property that is about to close escrow and you and everybody else is about to get paid—but wait, the market, the potential buyer, the seller or for any number of other reasons, the house will not sell at the price you thought it would. What to do? I know, the first thing we thing about is "the market shows the value" but before we do what is sooo easy and lazy to do- which of course is to drop the price 5, 10 of even up to 20k, let's see if we can come up with another solution.

How to Make More Money on Every Listing

We've talked about what to do to get a listing, what to do after you have the listing and how to execute the plan, and the proof that you've executed the plan to the homeowner. Maybe you're a crazy realtor and you agreed you would take a reduction in your commission if the house doesn't sell for what you initially agreed that it would sell for. (I've worked with these realtors) Maybe you want to make a little extra more, or maybe, just maybe you have gone through everything you can think of but the house still won't sell. But you don't want to take a reduction by dropping the price of the house; you want to get the highest amount of commission possible without having to drop the price. Here are some suggestions to get the highest dollar amount possible on any house:

Staging

One idea is staging, though staging is a like a standard for Realtors in some areas, it may be necessary if you have not already done it. Staging helps because it allows the avatar to see and feel what it's going to feel like to live in a home like that. Potential homeowners walk into homes and its cold, it's unattractive, but if you're able to put staging in there it would really make a difference and you may be able to sell the house faster.

Landscaping

Rather than throw a bunch of money into a new back deck, you could look out for some little things that you could use to improve the curb appeal and feel of the home. Something as simple as a flower box could improve the look and feel of the home, you could think of simple things like changing or painting the door, putting up a white fence; things that you could get cheaply. You could also take it to another level like placing a cute overhang over a doorway that needs character.

Think of cheap things that you could add. They don't even have to be permanent fixtures, they could be things you can use to beautify the home and when it sells you just pick them up and use them to sell the next house.

Present the Report of Renovations to the Buyer

If the house wouldn't sell and you've thought up all these ideas for renovations that would increase the appeal and sell ability of the home, go back to the potential buyers and let them know how much improvements and additions that you have done to the home. This way, they may be able to have a difference in opinion as to why they would buy the home. You could also offer warranties or guarantees for appliances in the home.

Appraisals

An appraisal is of course going to give you a lot of power behind the value of the home but this is best used when you know it will appraise. Maybe it doesn't have the awesome view as the other houses, or the corner lot. But if it will appraise, you can use that appraisal as ammunition. "Motivated seller must sell this week. Get it for 25% less then appraised value! Now of course, we can always extend that week and you're motivated because you want the buyer to think you're in a bind.

Increase the Buyers Agents Commission

You could increase the commission of the Realtor that is representing the buyer, by offering him more money in the form of commission, you're going to get more people looking at your house so when listing your home on MLS, there's a section that only agents can see. What you want to do is to say in the comment section *"I'm willing to pay an additional 1 percent commission to the buyer's agents".* What happens is that the buyer's agent would see this and is going to promote your own home over homes that may have similar attributes because he's going to get paid more.

He would show his client your home over any other competition because he's going to get paid a little bit more.

Creative Offers

Another strategy is creative offers. If you've done the open house you've done the questionnaire properly, you may have gotten a response that says *"This is great but I've got a suburban and the garage is so small, there's nowhere to fit that in"*. Rather than let these buyers walk away or rather than reduce the price of the house, you could make a crazy offer like: with a full price offer buyers would get a free car. Offer a smaller car that cost like seven thousand-dollars. So instead of reducing the price of the house by say, twenty-five thousand-dollars and you had a buyer who's interested but didn't get the house because he had a suburban, you could offer them a free smaller car. That means you took a seven thousand-dollars reduction as opposed to twenty-five thousand-dollars if you had to reduce the price and sell to a different buyer.

You're going to find out who your potential buyer is and what is keeping them from buying the house so that if it's something you can fix or add like maybe, putting a gate on the pool, or doing the landscaping in a way that they would like, you can.

You could ask them questions to know what they would want different and ask them if they would be willing to buy the home if you did it, this would help you decide what to offer.

They could even be things that you already have access to like maybe getting one of your contractors to fix something; paint the house, put carpet, put flooring, things that could be easily done.

I think just identifying what the buyers want through the questionnaire, you would be able to come up with all kinds of creative ways to make the home much more desirable to them. And if you look at the prices of these little things that you're going to have to put in place, it's definitely not going to cost you as much as a twenty-five thousand-dollars price reduction on the house. It could be appliances, refrigerator, gaming system, television, a water softener, a water heater; things that agents should have trusted people on-hand that can deliver for a fraction of the cost.

All these things are things that no one else is doing because a lot of Realtors are lazy and just go ahead to reduce prices when they can't sell the house because it's the home owner that really bears the cost when they do. So, the Realtor only has to bear a small fraction of the cost.

115

All of these are ways that you could get people interested in your offer and do something out of the ordinary, and what's important is that this is going to impress your homeowner that chose you as a listing agent. This is also going to attract more people to use you as their listing agent because you're talking about things that no one else is doing in the industry. Everybody is going to say "Wow, who is that guy?" because you are raising the standards in a way that hasn't been done before.

The Follow Up

WE FINALLY DID IT, THE HOUSE HAS SOLD! Whew, our job is done. Let's get paid, and move on already. Not so fast. For a customer, the day you close a sale is one of the happiest days of their lives. All the financials have gone through and all the documents have been signed. This is one of the biggest financial and likely an emotional moment of their lives and you've got the pleasure of making the call to let them know that their keys are waiting for them.

For most agents, this is where the relationship ends but this should be where the relationship should really start. You must let your client know this is not the end of your relationship with them but merely the beginning

This moment is hugely valuable. The very first thing you should let them know is "Thank you for putting your trust in me" Thank you so much for believing in me. You've got a lot of options out there but you chose me, thank you for letting me bring you to the finish line"

Right after you deliver the message, the person is pumped! Now is a very good time to get some materials you can use for marketing your business from them.

The most valuable thing that you can get from them at this point is a testimonial. This is a perfect time to ask for a testimonial; preferably by video and also by writing.

The best way to get it by video is to go hand-deliver the keys to them and ask for a few moments of their time. You could also ask them to meet you at their new house where you can then ask them for a video testimonial.

It is important to be aware of what to ask and how it should be scripted. I've got a document that I can share with you guys to show you how to develop the best script (what to say) that would get a client to say yes to your request for a video testimonial.

I've also got a spreadsheet that shows at least sixty ways that you can utilize a video testimonial in your business I will share with you. Remember that the client is in a very excited mood and would be more likely to oblige to your request.

You could deliver the keys to the home with a one hundred-dollar gift card to say *"Congratulations on your*

*home, thank you so much for putting your trust in me, and
here's a one hundred-dollars gift card to go get new keys
for the doors"*

You could even use this opportunity to create a signature
for yourself as an agent. For instance, every house that I
sell, I gift my clients with a touch pad key lock. It's like a
signature thing because from that anyone could easily tell
that the house was sold by me and also, whenever my
clients want to get into their home using their touch pad
locks, they would most likely think of me.

You could use anything, a fire alarm, home security
system, just make sure it is something that is not based on
taste and very practical.

That's a huge thank you I guarantee they are not expecting.
After delivering the gift card, the client will be more than
happy to comply with anything you may ask of them. What
else could you be after anyways? You already are getting
your payday. This is a perfect time to ask for the
questionnaire and testimonial.

The second thing you should do after obtaining that video
testimonial is to ask for a survey questionnaire. You could
do this through SurveyMonkey or any of the other

platforms out there that can be used to carry out customer surveys.

To keep itshort, I'm going to share at least 4 questions with you that you should include in your questionnaire. This is hugely valuable information so pay attention:

Question 1: Why Did You Choose To Do Business With Me?

They are going to answer with a number of reasons; some things you may be expecting and some things, you may not. What I've discovered is that the way they answer allows you to develop scripts that you can use when speaking with new clients.

For instance, if you ask a client *"Why did you do business with me"* and they go on to say that the reason is because you were truthful, truthful to the point that it was almost getting uncomfortable.

When talking to new clients, you can chip that in and let them know that people choose to do business with you because you are always truthful. You could add this in your pitch along with a link to the testimonials from your clients.

Question 2: What are Your Favorite Pastimes/ Hobbies?

This is a light-hearted question and they'll probably say something like: ", *I really enjoy going to the Lakers game, taking my kids to Disneyland, and going to Hawaii with my wife*"

This could give you an idea of what to offer your clients as gifts. In the next six months when it's their anniversary, you already have an idea of what gifts he would love; a paid excursion in Hawaii!! You could also do T-shirts, mugs, hats, etc. ; you can do basically anything themed around their hobbies.

Additionally, knowing their hobbies gives you an idea of how to connect with them on a more personal level.

Question 3: What Keeps You Up at Night?

The question you are asking here really is "*What is the one thing you wish would go away?*" and this is hugely valuable! Why? Because if you could identify what that is, and you are the guy or girl that may be able to solve the problem for them, you are a god-send!

If for instance, your client says that what keeps them up at night is a certain sickness that their child has and they don't have the resources to deal with it, you (or your virtual assistant) could do some research on your own about how to help them out, like maybe you find out a program that helps people deal with this disease. So for their next birthday, you could gift them with a ticket that admits the whole family to this program where they can learn how to deal with this issue. This gift is in-valuable.

Question 4: What Excites You or Motivates You?

This is a passion question. You are basically asking them what they look forward to doing every year. This is another opportunity for you to be able to deliver something amazing to them down the road. You could get them the tickets to a Christmas lights show that they look forward to attending every year. One note worth keeping in mind: Make sure to place the "What excites you or motivates you" right after the "what keeps you up at night". We don't want to get them in a downer mood. We are simply trying to see other ways in which we can genuinely help them again!

Keep in mind you have just delivered them the house of their dreams and they are very relieved at this point. You have a much better chance of getting truthful, straight-from-the-heart answers from them now more than any other time.

This should not be done before the sale or after the sale but on the exact day the deed has been recorded (its finalized the house is actually theirs).

This is a very important day to assert yourself as a marketer; whenever they remember that day, what plays back in their minds is not just *"I called my wife/husband/kids to tell them that we closed a house"* You are asserting yourself as a character in this movie and you are going to be embedded in the movie for the rest of their lives because you are a part of the movie now. They won't be able to get over the unique way that you delivered the news to them and they are going to want to tell everyone about it. You could also expand your part in their movie depending on your relationship you already have with them by taking them out for lunch or for dinner. But keep in mind you must know your customer well enough to know if you can take them out for lunch or dinner, you don't want to disrupt plans or impose. Then you'll call them and invite them to a celebratory lunch and talk about all the things that they could do in their new house. Again, you're inserting yourself into the movie.

At the lunch/dinner date, you can slide them that laminated paper we talked about of all the contacts of all the professional power players and people they could go to whenever they need anything or have any challenge concerning their new home. This is a list of contacts of the accountants, lawyers, plumbers, or any other service providers.

Circle of power suppliers

The circle of power suppliers are people you are working with in your industry or in your profession. These are people like gardeners, landscapers, carpenters, remodeling contractors, drywall installers, carpet cleaners, painters, and the handy man. They are people like that guy who sells home insurance, the refrigerator repairman, masonry guy, roofers, and garage door installers. These are people a homeowner would need if something needs to be fixed. I am talking about all the professionals who could help a homeowner get comfortable by having things sorted out and fixed if problems arise with the house.

When you client buys or sells a house, you will give the home buyer a list of these people. Whenever the home buyer needs help, they refer to the list you shared with them, and they can get in touch with the appropriate professionals to have the problem fixed. It's a directory of all the people you trust that can help the home buyer. These are people you recommend to the buyer because you know them and have worked with them in the past. They do a good job; they are trusted and won't mess up things during repairs or installations. You can say in the directory, "I have these guys work on repairs in my home, so I recommend them to you too." When you do this, you are obviously showing you care about the client and their home just as you would care about your own home.

When you set that friendship relationship with the circle powers, you are not only developing your real estate selling portfolio, but also understanding the kind of customers you relate with. It goes deeper than just having time together at the Opera, Disneyland, or Monster Jam event.

You are growing with your customers. It's a learning experience with a totally different sphere of influence. You are sharing a common interest based on preferences and the likes of your circle of powers. It's an opportunity for you for change. It allows you to grow professionally and personally.

THE DAY AFTER CLOSING:

Okay, so we made it through closing escrow, we even had delivered the keys, got the testimonial, got them to fill out the survey and even handed them a unexpected gift. We have officially done more than 99% of the realtors out there would ever do. BUT, how to do we make sure the clients are so freaking blown away they will NEVER forget us? Here is how:

Would a Realtor possible consider paying for the client's moving cost into a new home? Would he/she ever consider sending movers? Can a Realtor come personally with his kids to help the home buyer's family move? It is something not anyone is doing and would absolutely destroy the competition on the "my-realtor is cooler than your realtor" radar.

I know, no one enjoys moving because of the hassles, even me. It may be in the winter season, holidays, or other busy or inconveniencing times. However, helping a client to move in their new house can be done by paying for a portion of the cost of moving, you don't even have to be there personally- But I would recommend it (keep in mind these are great casual conversation starters! "Crazy how many people are moving right now...who else do you know that has kids going away to college right now?" You and I both know this is really asking the same thing as when you knock on someone's door and ask "do you know anyone looking to relocate?" But guess what, this environment, with this way of asking, will yield MUCHO better results.

Consider for example, a family just bought a new house, and the present location is just five miles away from the beautiful home. However, they have a house load of items that is troubling them to move. You can come in as a Realtor to help out. Ask them when they are moving and tell them you would like to help. It will [probably cost you around $500 for the movers.

Well, that may seem a lot but it is not. This is the client who can bring you thirty-thousand-dollars in a year. Does it hurt for you to spend five hundred-dollars dollars on this client? (Keep in mind, this will already is worked in your budget of how much "marketing dollars" you will be spending with this client)

Also, you can help in other ways by assisting them in solving small problems associated with moving to new locations. You probably know or can find out the best restaurants in the area. You can even surprise them by offering a special dinner at the restaurant on the day they move. This will turn the long, drawn out bad experience of moving into a nice beautiful ending. You not only have offered to help them move, but you have bought them dinner. They are going to want to move more often. The client will never forget you as a Realtor.

The small percent of the ten-thousand-dollars commission spent on moving, and the nice dinner treat give birth to a great deal of close to five referrals. This is the way to do business. But nobody wants to do that. No agent wants to spend that much. This is where the big business friendship line is drawn. If an agent offers that much to a client, it means he is leaving the business circle to friendship circle. This can bring huge changes in your real estate selling business. Try it out and you will see the results.

How about hosting something like a house warming party for the client? (This is an example of what you can do as a buyer's agent) What if you as the agent, hosted a house warming party after the clients get the keys to their new home? This is where you have the client invite ten people or friends and offer a flat-screen TV or X-box to the client? What if you host the party and offer something like a gift voucher to Disneyland or send them to the Bahamas? What would be a gift that would blow the customers away?

I think something extraordinary makes a great gift. Something associated with the house is always a safe bet. the clients can see the item and flashback about the experience of buying the home with you, like the flat-screen TV or the fancy BBQ. These are things can make a big impression to the buyer and other people attending the house warming party.

Go to all the neighbors in the area and meet the families with a "Hey, we are hosting a house warming party; would

you kindly join us at your new neighbor's home?"
Wouldn't that be a great invitation no matter who was
asking?

During the party, you can break out items like candles,
baked cakes, chocolate, flowers, and some other gifts just
to show the kind of appreciation you have for this client. At
that time, people are going to ask the home buyer, "Who
they heck is this guy?!"

The home buyer will of course, tell the neighbors and his
family that, "Dude, he is just my real estate agent!" This is
something no-one will be expecting. Even better, you are
going to be able to mingle and interact with these neighbors
during the house warming party. And you know what? If
you meet the neighbors in this atmosphere, it presents a
great opportunity for you as a Realtor to make yourself
known. And what better way to show who you really are?
Way better than a cheesy flyer with your face on it. You
may find out during this party the neighbors are seeking a
house to purchase for other family members, a friend, a
colleague, etc. and when you host this, you get a perfect
opportunity to inquire about those opportunities.

At the party, you bring a cooler with drinks for the party.
You will of course leave the cooler behind, it's part of the
gift and it will be a reminder for them. They will associate
it with you when they see the cooler in the house after you
left. You host a barbecue, and the neighbors, together with

your client, enjoy the food and drinks. It's a memorable experience and they don't have to spend a dime.

After that, do a follow up. Everything is about follow up. Take good shots of the party and design a portion of your newsletter surrounding this event. Then send it to the people on your list, make sure to name the people that were in attendance, people love to be mentioned in the press (even if it's just your press!). It will show how enjoyable the party was, and for those who didn't show, it will say "You missed it guys!" This is what we call social business— very powerful experience that can do magic in the selling business.

The surprise gifts they weren't expecting like the flat-screen TV or the BBQ will lure those who may be planning to buy a house to begin approaching you for a house. Maybe use this opportunity to bust out the Disneyland tickets. They will see you as the guy to deal with.

That client will post tons of photos in their social media with you in the car, at the ball game, at the airplane show or visiting the Opera— wherever you went with them during and after that treat. They will tell everybody about it. "What! Your agent did that?" "My agent doesn't do that, give me his number", "He is my new agent." That's a marvelous thing for a Realtor to do.

Regardless of the gift, make sure you allocate sometime for yourself to join them for the treat. You are piercing the friendship circle by doing it together. Its ten times more effective, not to mention tons of fun!

Hosting a house warming party also allows you to meet your customers outside the business environment— this is the friendship level. Just enjoying time with clients outside of business office makes a big difference. That's what the best Realtors do. It can change your life, change your business, and grow business support for years to come. All of this by just having a little fun outside of the office with your clients.

Now, let me ask; how many agents have a newsletter with something like hosting a house warming party where there was free food, drinks, and bar-b-ques and tickets? Do Realtors think along these lines? Not likely.

FOLLOW UP WEEKS AND MONTHS LATER

Now that we have wrapped up a few days of complete chaos with the closing and helping the clients move, we can relax a bit. But only a small bit. We've talked about the importance of follow-up and a good idea is to schedule calls to them once in a while. But it's very important to also ask over time if there is anything that has changed with their house good or bad…

It opens up an opportunity for you to discuss problems they may be having in their home. For instance, they could say the Plumber you recommended in your list has moved from the area. Then you could offer them a handyman or another plumber. Once again, you're the problem solver…hugely valuable!

Maybe you call 5 years down the road and they tell you of a problem you cannot immediately solve. Maybe there is going to be a construction of a new freeway on the other side of the house is located. Then you can begin to talk to them about the possibility of getting a new home. The usual response is going to be *"We can't afford it"* so you can tell them *"What if I can get you a new property for less than your payments are now?"* Then go ahead to connect them to a lender.

You are only able to do this when you are in contact with them because if you are not in contact with them, you wouldn't know of the problems they have and ultimately you can't have that opportunity to expand your relationship with them.

You could also connect with them by reminding them whenever any major service is due; Have an auto-email sent a week before their gutters should be cleaned (a certain date of the year that is typically when its needed) a reminder their home air filter needs to be replaced, or anything else that needs regular maintenance. In the email, you can include contact info for the professional that might be able to help with that service.

You want to blow their socks off? Pay for these things especially those services that don't cost much. Have the professional HVAC guy call the client and tell them "the service fee has already been taken care of by you, we just need a day and time that works best."

Keep in mind, If they're buying a house where you're making ten-thousand-dollars or twenty-thousand-dollars, you can pay for that because you know their friends are going to be on the same level and if you get referrals (which you would most certainly get if you do something special like this), you are able to make all what you have spent back.

To make things even easier, you could use a service like Amazon where you could pay to have things regularly delivered on a specific date you choose. So you could have new air filters or other stuff you know that they need, delivered to your client regularly without having to make extra efforts to remember it. Just pay it in advance, set the delivery dates and never have to worry about the reminders again.

One thing to think about when sending gifts: whenever you get a gift you can use or reuse, each time you do so, you think about the person who gifted it.

For instance, if you know your customer loves coffee and you buy them a fancy coffee maker, every time they make coffee.

If you send them a bottle of wine every month, every time they drink wine, they are going to be thinking of you and when they go buy wine, they are going to remember you.

It's just something we cannot get out of our head; we always think about who gave us the gift, subconsciously or consciously.

Think of it this way: If you give them a one-time use gift card, when they use it, they're going to think about you one time. But, if you buy them something they can use every day, they are going to think about you every day! Whatever it is; it could be a T-shirt, it could be a hat; whenever they wear that hat, they're going to think about you.

These are just some marketing strategies that create an emotional connection to your client through gifts. This might look like spending a lot of money but the whole idea behind this marketing strategy is to pay for the marketing in a way like no other realtor is doing, also one that you will likely benefit waaayy more from. After the relationship has been built, you and the client will be benefiting from the gifts.

Imagine it's a birthday gift. You call one of your clients and tell them you are taking them to a motorcycle track; it will only take an hour to sort all the business items. This is another great way to extend your interaction with the client. But this is not what Realtors are doing. What Realtors are thinking is just because they sold a house to a client, they deserve more business from that person. That's not customer relationships management. That is entitlement.

Heck, when you hand deliver these gift items to them, you could take selfies or photos you could use as part of your marketing material. Other potential clients can see all the things they can benefit from doing business with you!

Again, you must understand this is not expensive because we are talking of a pre-set marketing budget based on money you have already received and you've already determined that this is the amount of money you are going to devote to marketing to obtain a new deal. It's not an out-of-pocket expense, its money that comes from a committed budget.

If you're making five thousand-dollars on a deal and you already know you're going to spend five hundred –dollars of that on getting another deal, this is all part of the five hundred -dollars. If all your efforts turn into another deal you could make another five thousand-dollars from the five hundred -dollars that you invested in your marketing budget.

The cycle goes on and on and you have everything to gain and nothing to lose.

Where to Go from Here

Before we start about the next steps to take, let's
summarize what we have learned so far.

We began by identifying what the norm is: what the normal
compensation for agents is (both on a national and local
level), what the normal amounts of transactions are, and
what the normal marketing is…the consensus: it's all
BORING and quite frankly disappointing.

We then gave a small example of what it looks like when
you do things different. This was the story I shared with
you about when I called a top performing agent for the first
time. She made me feel like I was the most important
person in the world at that very moment. In that time of my
life, I started to think: this is how it should be done! This is
also appropriately where the book shifted into the new way
of thinking.

We discussed being a successful realtor truly is easier than
you think. It's actually really fun, because it's about being
less of an "agent" and really more about being someone fun
to hang out with. This is marketing in a way that no one
else is really doing in this business and it attracts clients to
you like crazy.

Pop quiz: do you remember how to figure what the average value of a customer is, as well as the average lifetime value of a customer? If you don't, you HAVE to go back and read this section (page 28). It's very important! This information tells us how much to invest in marketing, where to direct your efforts, the amount of time it will involve and with who to do it with. This ultimately will dictate how you schedule and plan your days.

Creating your marketing plan is huge! It began with a brief intro to personal marketing including an elevator pitch and short video. Remember to be yourself, and have fun. People like to be around others that don't look like machines. The purpose of this elevator pitch and video is to not have it perfect, but to have it. Small variations are fine, even preferred! Just have fun creating this and be yourself.

Then we got into the meat of it: business marketing. Within the business marketing plan, we took you through what it means to create S.M.A.R.T goals. You need a personal goals as well as professional; how much money do you need to retire? Exactly how many months do you need to work for? How many homes do you need to sell in order to reach that goal? In this section of the book we answered those questions.

Then we took you through how to identify your target market using the nifty-difty avatar assignment I will be sharing with you.

We then spoke about ways to generate new business from just a few examples from a list of about 85 ways I will give to you. These few examples included networking, creative business cards, utilizing some cool door knocking techniques and even using the circle of other professionals you already deal with every day.

After you have a prospect, it's important to know who the end buyer will be right out of the gate. In this section of the book we discussed the importance of being able to qualify the lead so you know how to approach the situation and what the exit strategy will be before you even consider moving forward.

How do we get to keep the deal flow coming in? This portion of the book is dedicated to really digging into the referral strategy (Something that for the most part, no one in R.E. is doing!) It's important to understand the mechanics of the referral system including the budget, how to create your bomb-shell power referral package and the very special ways to say thank you to that special someone: your client.

After a house doesn't sell for the price either you or the client believes it will sell for, the knee-jerk reaction is to drop the price right? The market will show is the true value right? Wrong. In this section, I give you a plethora of items to throw a wrench in that thought pattern and avoid the "let's just drop it 10k and get rid of this sack of potatoes" mentality. Keep the client happy, gain more business once your clients and others see your level of creative thinking, possibly get a higher price for the property and put more money in your pocket!

In the very last part of the book, we talk about the most important part of being a real estate agent: continually building the relationship. In *normal* (remember this whole book is about being non-normal) circumstances, you would for the most part end the relationship after closing. As a homeowner, I can say very rarely are there many instances of communication other than the occasional thank you card, email, or phone call asking if I, or anyone I know looking for another home. LAME

Ladies and gentlemen, believe me when I say this: The follow up is not only the most important part of this book, but the most undervalued part of real estate sales as we know it! This is the part of the business that is a non-negotiable, it has to be done! Get to know your clients, have fun with them, communicate with them and stay in contact with them. People do business with people.

Generally, they do it with people they know, like and trust. Be that person for many other people, and you will be able to make tital waves in this business.

You may be thinking to yourself right now: Ok Jeb, we just went through a whirl-wind of information. I have no clue where to start or what to even think about all of this. What about something I can use immediately, like today? That's exactly what I'm going to give you in the last section of this book; some things that you can use today, right away. The things I am about to talk to you about will help you no matter what you do in life, it will ensure success follows you everywhere. Here you go:

Creating the jump start to success

It starts with creating a better version of you. The most success I have had in this industry has come as a direct result of how much I have invested in myself. It's not about how much I have invested in doing real estate but in personal development courses. It's about how much one can absorb from the lessons learned by others. It's very important to actively and constantly pursue personal development. Start with something like surrounding yourself with likeminded individuals that want more. These types of people want more out of there business, out of there career, more for their families, more out of life. Jim Rohn (motivational Speaker) once said: *"You are the*

141

average of the 5 people you spend the most time with"
While there are many versions of this quote, the premise is
all the same. Hang out with people that are better then you,
and you will naturally become a better person. They lift
you up!

Currently, I am involved with four different masterminds.
What's incredible about most of these masterminds is that
we're groups or a collection of successful individuals that
are in all different industries.

In its simplest form, a mastermind is group of people who
come together and collectively brainstorm on how they
could handle and overcome situations in a certain business.
In this context, a mastermind stands for a batch of smart
people getting together in a room sharing ideas,
information, and solving problems. These are like the board
of directors. This is definitely a good start for finding
people that will lift you to becoming a better version of
yourself. (As a matter of fact, most of my motivation to
write this book was from the support I received from
people in these groups!)

Because I'm in several mastermind groups, it is like I have
multiple boards of directors, all giving their own pieces of
invaluable advice. Each group has a different number of
members. The larger group primarily consists of
professionals in the real estate industries that meet about

four times a year. The smaller group meets about once a week, but this group consists of individuals in diverse industries which deliver a very different value then the larger one with only real estate professionals.

So, I have been hanging around with successful people not only in real estate but in virtually all industries. These are people who have become successful in their respective industries and now they are sharing with me information and insight about business where it has taken them sometimes several decades to discover. This is something unimaginable— working with people from different industries who have tried different strategies, learned from their failures and from there mistakes and now they are sharing all that information with you. As you can see, getting involved with a mastermind or any other type of event or meeting place on a regular basis to collectively overcome challenges is a huge catapult in creating success, no matter what industry you are in.

So, if you are a real estate agent and you are not in any mastermind group, then it means you are likely doing things like the 'normal' agent. You really need to find a mastermind group or accountability partner. I'm not talking about networking groups (which these have their own specific value) I'm talking about someone that is going to put you on the 'hot-seat'. Someone who is going to help you dig into your business so you can work on your business, not in it. This way, you will start getting ideas about what is working and not working and what strategies can be applied to real estate in general and more specific, your book of business. That's how to be 'not normal' in real estate selling. That my friends is what you would call a life-hack.

AUDIO BOOKS

Another thing you can do to further personal development is listen to audio books. Whenever I turn on my car, I listen to audio books. I don't listen to a radio in my car; it might as well be disconnected. As long as my vehicle is moving, I'm listening to an audio book.

I actually have dozens of queued-up books in my audio files on my phone. They play continuously and as soon as I finish one book, another starts playing. I mostly listen to personal development books with authors like Jim Rohn, Grant Cardone, Napoleon Hill. I also like to switch it up and listen to other books running the gambit from Merlin the Wizard to a book by Oprah (yes ma, I read her book).

You can do it while you drive, walk, workout or swim—there is no excuse. It takes away the hurdles you cross when you start a book, but can't finish it because you don't have time.

Reading a book will require you to set up the right conducive environment— somewhere quiet and free of distractions. However, when it comes to audios, you can do them anywhere.

This is how I have managed to blast through tons of books— For me, going the audio route is much easier than the traditional route. But here is the thing: I know there are those of you out there that just *love* to curl up next to the fire with a cup of hot chocolate and your favorite blanket and just read a good book. Well, that's not me. And that's not what we're talking about here. We're talking about hammering out books like they are those really small lunch size bags of potato chips you get from Costco. As soon as you start, they are already done and you're like…That's it? Dang, you better hand me another one of those.

Audible is a great platform for this audio book style of reading. It allows you to download books so you don't have to be hooked up to the internet to be able to listen, and on top of that, I found a pretty cool trick. Audible has got an option where you can speed up or slow down the rate in which you listen to an audio book. So, you can listen to the book faster then normal. What's really interesting about this is that we can listen MUCH faster than we can talk and most deftly faster than we can read. Want to get though the same book your friend has been reading for the last 4 months done in four days? Listen to books at 2x speed (sometimes 2.5 depending on the speaker) like I do, it may sound funny at first having the person sounding like he just sucked off of a helium balloon, but trust me nobody's laughing when they hear you just took down a book the size of an Encyclopedia in 4 days. All of a sudden things get serious: "There is no way you can do that!". But now you know there is. It's called another life hack.

One thing to think about when selecting your audio book: Sometimes you are listening to an audio book but you are not completely engaged. Just like good music, what you need to do is find a book that is perfect for any given situation. For example, you're listening to the book *10X Rule* by Grant Cardone heading to the gym, it's like listening to the Rocky soundtrack but in book form rather than Music. Cardone has the tenacity and energy to get you stirred up.

On the other hand, you may be reading the book *Getting Things Done* by David Allen while at home on your computer; this is a good opportunity to take notes and stay more connected on very focused level. Ensure you pick the right audio book given a particular situation. Some audio books are a lot more engaging and you need to be more focused. The reason being, you are not in same state of mind all the time.

Start with these small "life-hacks" to give your everyday life a jumpstart into high gear. Then, once you have joined an accountability group you will begin to see that this is only the beginning of a journey to happiness and success. (Yes I know it sounds cliché, but it's the truth!) Start with personal development and you will see it really is the slingshot for growing your business. Ask almost anyone who is really successful in the industry. It's almost like in order to get to the next level of success in business, or in order to become more successful at your job, career or at life in general, you have to first become a better version of yourself. And that my friends, is only gained through personal development.

I just shared with you just a couple of the things that have helped me in the world of personal development and I hope it was helpful and can be useful to you and your career. I want to thank you for reading this book, for knowing that by reading this book and actively applying the methods, techniques, and systems within the pages you will gain 10x income, and for understanding the current way things are being done in this industry is outdated, boring, normal and will likely get you nothing more than a couple gold stars next to your name if you stick in it long enough. I don't know about you, but I never wanted the gold stars next to my name in school, I wanted what the gold stars got me: freedom from the race, from the competition and from the average results.

You now have the key...NOW GO GET IT!

To your unbelievable and yet still attainable success,

Jeb Durgin